FEAR NO MAN

GEORGE REED
WITH DAVE HUNT

HARVEST HOUSE PUBLISHERS
Eugene, Oregon 97402

Scripture quotations are taken from the King James Version of the Bible.

FEAR NO MAN

Copyright © 1987 by George Reed and Dave Hunt
Published by Harvest House Publishers
Eugene, Oregon 97402

Library of Congress Catalog Card Number 86-080712
ISBN 0-89081-541-0

Printed in the United States of America.

*This book is dedicated
with deepest respect to my father,
Edwin W. Reed,
whose influence has been basic
to my entire philosophy of life.
Although I watched him closely, not once
did he compromise his inner convictions
and personal ethics. He was a leader of men—
mentally, physically, and spiritually.
He feared God but feared no man.*

Acknowledgments

Soon after retiring from the United States Board/Commission of Parole on January 31, 1978, I decided to reduce my experiences of nearly a quarter of a century in the nation's capital into a book. I strongly desired to interpret 23 years of American history at the vortex of power. My years administering the Federal Criminal Justice System, either as Chairman or Vice-Chairman of the United States Board/Commission of Parole, gave me an inside picture of my beloved America, its people, its government, and its strengths and weaknesses.

I am profoundly grateful to my coauthor, Dave Hunt, for his ability to grasp my dream from the beginning and for his skill at polishing my story, FEAR NO MAN. He added great strength to the text and helped make my life experiences come alive.

I am particularly grateful to Eileen L. Mason, Editor-in-Chief of Harvest House Publishers, for her enthusiasm toward the project and for the legal advice and support of Norman G. Juggert in his tireless efforts to cause the book to meet all federal and state legal requirements.

I am deeply indebted to my longtime friend and Chief Legal Counsel, the Honorable Joseph Barry, and his legal aid, Herman Levi, of the United States Board of Parole, for wise legal advice for some 20 years.

To my sweetheart of nearly 50 years, Lois, who always encouraged me, typed, and sometimes corrected my memory of our history; for her patience, help, and most of all her confidence that I could complete the job—my heartfelt thanks.

To my son, George Calvert, daughter-in-law, Jane, and grandsons, Jesse and Joel, for their inspiration and support in desiring that these pages of history be honest, accurate, and complete—my love and deep appreciation.

Foreword

Reading the manuscript FEAR NO MAN was as compelling as anything I have ever read. Once starting to read I had to discipline myself to put it down. The content is filled with information and inspiration communicated in a most readable way.

Dr. George J. Reed had a colorful and an unusually significant role during some exceedingly critical, dangerous days in American history. His initiatives in criminology have ramifications for years to come. As I read, it seemed like George was addressing the whole issue of criminology in all of its ramifications and complications as it is being faced today. He was "prophetic" in his concern and his solutions.

It was my pleasure to know George Reed as a personal friend during some of his most difficult days. It was then I learned of his strong faith so rooted in Christ and the scriptures. As a pastor whose primary conviction was that the greatest influence for Christ in history is through the laity, not the preachers, George Reed was a model and an example one could wish would be emulated by all laity. He wrote and spoke and worked as one constrained by the love of God and accountable to him in everything.

This book records a remarkable career in an area of concern more critical and explosive today than it was during the time about which he writes. Seeing this monumental problem through the eyes of one with his credentials, his experience, and his faith is especially illuminating, inspiring and challenging.

This is a book for which the time has come. It will be of interest to those mildly curious about the whole field of criminology. It will be a guide and a profound resource for those who are committed to criminology in its broadest scope. It will be unexpectedly rewarding and compelling to the casual reader.

—Dr. Richard C. Halverson
Chaplain of the United States Senate

Contents

1
Farewell to Camelot

Don't let it be forgot
That once there was a spot,
For one brief shining moment,
That was known as Camelot.

Camelot! There was a strange magic about that legendary place. What was the secret of its haunting hold on human imagination? Was it more than fiction? Prophetic, perhaps? Who could fail to see that dazzling splendor materializing out of the past, complete with mystical aura, on the banks of the Potomac! "For one brief shining moment. . . ." Prophetic indeed—more so than any of us who were part of it had suspected. We couldn't believe it when the end came so suddenly.

Was it only coincidence, or some mysterious quirk of fate, that the captivating musical had been a smash hit on Broadway just before the inauguration of John Fitzgerald Kennedy? Whatever the cause, the new President felt a strange identity with the music and lyrics that never failed to move him deeply. Often at the end of an exhausting day, whether in the White House or traveling, Kennedy would listen once again to its compelling magic. Was it only an understandable attempt to escape momentarily the overwhelming pressures of his responsibilities, a proven way to relax? Or was his identification with Camelot a glaring symptom of the deadly delusion that blinds all of us to the real life-and-death significance hidden in the events swirling about us?

Knowing the new President's fascination with Camelot, political writers had persisted in finding real and imagined parallels between this ancient tale and the Kennedy Administration. Some ridiculed him as a naive Prince Charming, whose liberal theories would ruin the country. Others accused him of being an impractical idealist, whose dreams would never work in the real world. Most younger Americans, however, saw in JFK a champion who shared their hopes for a new world and would turn them into reality.

The musical ended with King Arthur singing the lilting chorus that the President loved so well. He would lean back and close his eyes. Indeed, he was a dreamer—and his dreams of a modern Camelot had inspired all of us who shared that brief but shimmering era in the nation's capital. Years before, his father, Joseph Kennedy, wealthy ambassador to the royal court of King Arthur's successors in England, had reportedly said that he would spend 20 million dollars to put his son Jack in the White House. How much he actually spent, and how important those millions were in attaining that determined goal, and what was accomplished thereby, are still matters for speculation.

Arriving in Washington with all the trappings of royalty, John Fitzgerald Kennedy had regally refurbished the presidential mansion, including its guards and the Marine Band. In a final touch reminiscent of a scene from

Camelot, he had installed trumpeters on the White House steps. The Kennedy family and the young, confident team that surrounded the President exuded an aura of wealth, power, pomp, high society, and excited optimism that swept over Washington immediately after the inauguration. The fond memory of this modern "King Arthur" with his beautiful "Queen Guinevere" at his side, and the outstanding corps of young idealists that helped to make what came to be known as the "Imperial Presidency," still returns to haunt us with questions of what might have been, if only. . . .

There was a transformation, not only of the political climate on Capitol Hill, but of Washington society as well. Even the most hardened veterans in the halls of power succumbed eventually to the charm of the new First Lady, whose special touch influenced the seat of government in subtle ways. Jackie Kennedy introduced a new sense of glamour and gaiety that all of Washington eagerly sought to emulate and enjoy. Overnight the White House took on the air of a legendary court that seemed better suited to Europe than to America. Most remarkable of all was the mystique of unconquerable optimism that captivated all of us on the The Hill. An overpowering sense of destiny is the only way to describe it.

No mere Prince Charming, John F. Kennedy was an able administrator, a skillful and inspiring leader. In a deadly confrontation that would have severely challenged the most experienced and capable head of state, the dashing young President of the United States held a firm course during the Berlin crisis. The Soviets then gambled on an even more dangerous test. I shall never forget how Washington came to a full military alert almost in a moment. The young "king" was out campaigning for a senator in the Midwest when he suddenly returned to Washington with a "cold." Intelligence had confirmed the presence of Soviet nuclear missiles in Cuba. True to his *Profiles in Courage*, John Fitzgerald Kennedy took us right to the brink of nuclear war to call the Soviet bluff. At the eleventh hour Khrushchev backed down—but not without exacting a promise that the United States would stop its sponsorship of military actions against Cuba by Cuban exiles, most of whom operated brazenly out of Miami's "Little Havana." Few of us gave that arrangement much thought until it was too late.

The low point in the Kennedy presidency had come with the embarrassing failure of the ill-conceived invasion, attempted by Cuban exiles (backed, as it turned out, by the CIA with JFK's approval) to liberate Fidel Castro's island from Communism. Poor intelligence had badly underestimated the wily dictator's strength and had given naive credence to the unrealistic hope of a popular uprising of the oppressed people against him. As a consequence, a pitifully inadequate force of invaders had been committed to a fantasy mission that had been doomed to complete failure before it began.

There were rumors that JFK had promised air and naval support to the attackers, and then withdrawn it at the last moment after the invasion was already under way. Whatever the true facts, eventually President Kennedy had shouldered the blame for the disastrous adventure, and the distasteful memories of the Bay of Pigs fiasco gradually faded into the past. Except for a few insiders, there were not many of us in Washington who even suspected that in spite of promises to Khrushchev, JFK and his brother Bobby were continuing a secret CIA-sponsored espionage war against Cuba. Whether this actually included the rumored plots to assassinate Fidel Castro or not, the continued activities and boasts of numerous exile groups with headquarters in "Little Havana" gave enough substance to the stories to form a basis for retaliation by Castro and his Soviet overlords. Such a suggestion, however, was too fantastic for any of us in Washington to have taken it seriously. Such things simply couldn't happen at Camelot.

It was quietly whispered that the CIA maintained a secret Caribbean navy for continuing sorties along the Cuban coast by frogmen and commandos. When in port, its flagship, a converted 174-foot subchaser renamed the *Rex*, allegedly docked only a short distance from the Kennedy family's Palm Beach estate. JFK reportedly had been furious upon learning that the *Rex* had been there during one of his vacation visits. In late October of 1963, a *Rex* landing party of Commandos Mambises, apparently betrayed by a double agent, was ambushed as it neared a prearranged rendezvous. The sudden glare of searchlights and flares turned a dark night into day, exposing the special black-rubber rafts with silent-running outboard motors speeding up the small mouth of a Cuban coastal river. In a moment, as the commandos opened fire and wheeled around desperately to escape, the overwhelming firepower of Castro's "reception committee" turned the river red with the blood of the dead and dying.

After playing hide-and-seek with Cuban gunboats for several days along the Yucatan Peninsula, the *Rex* eventually escaped. Castro waited patiently until his elusive quarry had slipped quietly back into its dock near the Kennedy family estate in Palm Beach. Then, on the night of October 30, 1963, Fidel held a live news conference on Havana's television station CMQ. In self-righteous tones, the wily dictator accused the United States of continuing acts of war against Cuba. He described the CIA flagship down to the minutest detail of its special electronic gear, and told where it could be found at that very moment. He then put in front of the cameras four captured Commandos Mambises, survivors of the recently ambushed raiding party. With prompt-ings from Castro, they made their "confessions" to the world and were rewarded for their "honesty" with 30-year prison terms. In Washington, rumors flew, including speculations about brainwashing, torture, and false confessions. Those who knew the truth kept a close-lipped silence, including White House Press Secretary Pierre Salinger, whose only comment was "no comment."

Publicly, President Kennedy seemed oblivious to Castro's damning accusations. He was busily pressing for enactment of his package of civil rights legislation, hoping it would bring relief from the violent uprisings that had erupted across the nation in some of the largest black ghettos. Those of us serving in Washington were convinced that by the 1964 elections the tarnished dream of the New Frontier would have once more assumed its lost luster. Camelot was still alive, and would be with us for another four-year term.

So we thought, unaware that our young "king" was about to keep an appointment with sudden and violent death. In later perspective, some of us would, in spite of the Warren Report, cautiously voice the suspicion that Oswald had not acted alone, but that Khrushchev and Castro had gotten their revenge. Such speculations, how-ever, were carefully silenced at the beginning to prevent a grieving populace from making an outcry for retalia-tion that might have precipitated a third world war.

Caught up in the glory of the present, I couldn't even suspect the horror creeping over the horizon. I was in a euphoric mood on that memorable Wednesday, Novem-ber 20, 1963, as I drove homeward after a very heavy day of parole hearings at the Justice Department. Three weeks earlier, my wife, Lois, and I had received a heavily

embossed invitation that I still have among my most prized mementos. This was by no means our first White House reception, nor would it be the last, but—farthest from our thoughts at the time—it would be our final opportunity to share in the glory that was Camelot. Engraved in gold beneath the President's seal shone the following words:

The President and Mrs. Kennedy
request the pleasure of the company of
Mr. & Mrs. Reed
at a reception to be held at
The White House,
Wednesday evening, November 20, 1963
at six-thirty o'clock.

Washington's nightly exodus of bureaucrats fleeing for the suburbs generates such horrendous traffic jams that each one seems more impossible than the last. November 20 was no exception, and anticipation of the exciting festivities that I would soon participate in made me more impatient than usual. Driving at a slow crawl across the Roosevelt Bridge in bumper-to-bumper traffic, I performed my evening ritual of mentally throwing all parole cases out the window and into the Potomac River. Early in my career I had firmly decided that I couldn't afford to take home with me the twisted lives of prisoners I had been dealing with, accompanied by the emotional tug-of-war between sympathy for their spouses and families and concern for the danger that their parole could bring to the public. Throwing these burdens into the Potomac each evening was a deliberate exercise of the will. No matter that next morning I would just as deliberately resurrect those same tragic complexities and carry them back to work with me.

My good friend and fellow Parole Board member, Gerald Murch, with his lovely wife, Fiona, beside him, fought the evening traffic back into Washington to the White House while I relaxed in the rear seat with my wife, Lois. Pulling into the East Gate with a few minutes to spare, Gerald handed the Secret Service guard our special identification. As always on such occasions, the security was extremely tight. Even the mail was not trusted. Each invitation had been hand-delivered to our homes. Following the East Driveway across the White House grounds, Gerald pulled up to the designated entrance, where we left the car under the large overhang. After our invitations and identity were checked once again by Secret Service agents, we entered the presidential mansion.

This was the annual reception for the President's judiciary appointees, one of seven similar functions hosted by the President and First Lady each fall. Such events were *always* formal, with white ties and tails for the men and long gowns for the women. But this one was going to be different. For the first time ever in my experience at a White House reception, dress had been designated as semiformal. It was to be a fun, relaxed sort of party, so unusual for Camelot.

Checking hats and coats, we moved past the cloakroom and through a long hall into the passageway that connects the East Wing with the main part of the White House. Secret Service agents were conspicuous everywhere— alert, fit, discreet. Ascending to the main floor, we entered the Great Hall of the White House, where we joined a growing crowd of federal judges and other judicial leaders and their ladies. Carrying on a tradition begun by George Washington, the President's own Marine Band, in brilliant red-and-gold braid, was already setting the tone for the evening with lively dinner music.

"The floral arrangements are exquisite!" murmured Lois softly, giving my arm a squeeze. I knew that this simple remark was intended to convey much more that she couldn't put into words: that inexpressible sense of awe that always overwhelms even the most hardened political veterans when confronted by the pomp and glory surrounding the leader of the most powerful nation on earth. Trying to rein in the rising excitement that I too felt, I nodded my appreciation of the unusually beautiful yellow-and-gold blooms that filled the large hall with brilliant fall color.

Greeting old friends and casual acquaintances, we moved slowly with the swelling crowd into the magnificent Gold Room. One could feel the mounting sense of expectancy. There was a momentary pause in the music . . . then suddenly the Marine Band struck up "Hail to the Chief!" Three hundred pairs of eyes turned to the broad staircase. Right on cue, the President appeared, with Jacqueline on his arm. Smiling happily, exuding that special Kennedy charm, they descended the stairs in as grand an entrance as ever Arthur and Guinevere had made. Behind them swept the lords and ladies of the realm—from Vice President Lyndon B. Johnson and his Ladybird to Chief Justice and Mrs. Earl Warren, other justices of the Supreme Court, and Cabinet members and their wives.

While the Marine Band played on, we, the lesser members of the court, followed into the State Dining Room, where a delicious buffet was waiting. As we ate, the conversation at every table ran the gamut of political concern: the reception which the President's program was receiving on The Hill, who the leading purveyors of power were that controlled the fate of specific bills, what bills were likely to pass in the next session, and the

President's coming trip to Texas to mend political fences with conservatives who were blocking the implementation of his New Society. International politics, especially the enigmatic Kremlin, was of course a topic of interest, as was the latest gossip about social figures, parties, and press releases concerning Washington's elite society. I had not been able to escape the implications of the two meanings of the same word, but for tonight I was content to savor the apparent identity of "high society" and the "New Society."

It takes no medical training to detect the advanced stages of "Potomac Fever" among the guests at such occasions. Indeed, I felt the flush of that contagious malady in my own face, and I could see it in Lois and even some symptoms in Gerald and Fiona Murch, who were as close to immune as one could be. No one who comes to Washington to fill even the most obscure appointment is likely to escape this indigenous disease. It infects to some degree nearly everyone who becomes even a minor custodian and dispenser of the near-absolute power generated in a nation's capital. Life at the vortex has a dizzying effect that turns even the coolest heads at times.

When the last glass had been raised, we followed our host and hostess into the ballroom, where leading stars of *West Side Story* and other Broadway hits recreated a few moments of Broadway glitter. We then enjoyed an informal time of repartee between the President and some of the more distinguished guests. Afterward, the Marine Band struck up, and the Ballroom floor was soon alive with swirling couples. When Supreme Court Justice William O. Douglas, who was nearing 70, swept onto center stage, whirling his 19-year-old bride and third wife in a fast step, every head turned in their direction, and for a long and breathless moment the crowded floor seemed to belong only to them. Had it not been for Douglas's white hair, the two would have looked like high school sweethearts as they danced in close embrace. Justice Douglas and his attractive wife represented not only the two extremes of life—age and youth—but also of the legal profession: he at the very top, she just starting college. Eventually he would help her through law school.

Having made our way slowly through the reception line, where we greeted the guests of honor, my longtime friend and fellow Parole Board member, Richard Chappell, and I decided to look in on the Green Room. To our surprise, we found it empty. Under the somber gaze of former Presidents Woodrow Wilson and Abraham Lincoln, Richard and I sat down briefly, facing the large fireplace. Both of us commented upon the uniquely laid firewood. Was its arrangement the subject of a regular morning briefing in the housekeeping offices? Because the fireplace had not been lighted, we wondered aloud who took care of such a mundane affair as ordering when a fire would or would not be lit in any of the many fireplaces scattered throughout the White House. Had we chanced upon a missing link in the chain of command? Were there other missing links more serious?

Abruptly my good friend, who has an irrepressible sense of humor, turned to me and said in a very serious tone, "Mr. President, I have just returned from my assignment as Ambassador to Australia, and I wish to report, Sir, that we have never had a better relationship with our good friends *down under*!"

Willing on an impulse to play along with his game, particularly since he had cast me in the role of President, I replied pompously: "Ambassador Chappell, this improved relationship with our powerful ally is most gratifying. It was because of your courtly Southern

Georgia diplomacy that I named you to this most important post. You have exceeded my fondest imagination in carrying out your assignment. The entire nation is indebted to you . . . ."

My voice trailed off as Richard Chappell and I simultaneously sensed the presence of someone else in the room. Turning with an embarrassed grin, I saw one of the White House porters standing just inside the room and staring wide-eyed. He seemed genuinely awestruck to have stumbled upon such a high-level conference. We burst out laughing, and eventually I convinced him that Chappell was no more the Ambassador to Australia than I was the President of the United States and that I didn't even have a desire to take on that awesome responsibility.

Remembering the long-standing tradition that the Chief Executive and First Lady retire to their living quarters on the second floor at 11:00 P.M. without exception, I glanced at my watch. It was 10:45. Already, because of the lateness of the hour, the President was making his way toward the elevator, and the reception line was in a state of flux, breaking off in one place and reassembling in another as he moved through the crowd, shaking hands and pausing for a brief word here and there as he went. By a fortuitous shift in the President's path, I found myself among the last to shake his hand and thank him for the evening's hospitality. Little did I realize what that memory would mean to me in just a few days!

Pausing in front of the elevator, President Kennedy looked around, searching the crowd for Jacqueline. At last he saw her not far away, engrossed in last-minute conversation with a tight little group of attentive women. Turning to some of us who were standing nearby, he winked and said, "Fellows, I have to wait on my wife, too!"

The President stood there in mock impatience, holding

the elevator door open with his left hand. Hurrying up at the last minute, Jackie ducked under his outstretched arm and into the elevator. I caught a fleeting glimpse— the last one I would ever have—of these two standing together as the door slid shut. Glancing at my watch, I noticed that it was exactly 11:00 P.M.

The drive home that night was lighthearted. We laughed and shared anecdotes and agreed that we liked the new informality. It hadn't diminished any of Camelot's charm at all. We were unabashedly proud of our young, virile, and capable leader. There would be other such evenings. There would be a second term, possibly even a third. And we would ride the crest with him.

It was a short night for the President and his party. At 6:00 A.M. the helicopter lifted off from the South Lawn and headed for its connection with Air Force One at Andrews Air Force Base. Vice President Lyndon B. Johnson was an important part of the entourage, for he would be a key participant in his home state of Texas in the political fence-mending which the President hoped to accomplish with Democratic party leaders. That night the presidential party stayed at a hotel in Fort Worth, Texas, near the Dallas-Fort Worth airport. Already the trip promised to be a great success, and the President was in understandably high spirits when he at last turned in.

The following day, Friday, November 22, 1963, dawned crisp and clear. From Fort Worth, the Kennedys made a brief flight to Love Field in Dallas, where they moved quickly into the waiting White House limousine, to be joined by Governor Connally and his wife. Insisting upon being in full view, the President refused the safety of a roof and bulletproof glass. He wanted the fullest exposure to the Dallas crowd and to the millions who would watch on television. The Secret Service acquiesced with scarcely an objection.

The events of the next few moments would be forever emblazoned on the hearts and minds of most of the civilized world. At 12:30 P.M., as the President's car took its fateful turn in front of the Texas School Book Repository, the deadly sound of rifle fire suddenly silenced the cheering. For the crowd lining the street and those watching on television, joy turned to unbelieving horror. In that microcosm of suspended time no one knew whence the shots had come, but the President had fallen forward, and Governor Connally also seemed to have been hit. The heart-rending sight of Jackie Kennedy in the back seat bravely trying to shield the President as the driver accelerated to make a futile dash to the Parkland Hospital for medical attention was viewed by a stunned nation and world as it happened. Those who watched would never forget that sight.

At the time I was neither watching television nor listening to the radio, so was unaware of the tragedy which had just transpired. In the middle of a busy day, I had determined to clear my mind by getting out of the office. Returning from a quick lunch, I was driving down Constitution Avenue when a friend pulled alongside. "Have you heard the President's been shot?" he shouted.

"No!" I yelled back in disbelief. "Are you sure?"

The anguish in his eyes as he nodded and drove on convinced me that the story was true. By the time I reached the Justice Department, all doors were locked and guarded. Only those people with official business and Department I.D. were allowed inside. Already the armed forces were on full alert. Attorney General Robert F. Kennedy, the President's brother, was under heavy guard, as were members of the Cabinet. Entering through the private parking lot for Department personnel, I hurried upstairs to the newsroom across the hall from the Attorney General's office. A stunned crowd had gathered around the teletype machines that carried news services, waiting and hoping against hope to the end. Going reluctantly to my office at last to keep an appointment, I found everyone there clustered around a radio, keeping an anxious vigil to see whether the stricken President would live or die. Still, in those sad eyes and subdued voices there was a resignation that said it was hopeless.

A few hours later, a mourning and still unbelieving nation watched on television as Federal Judge Sarah T. Hughes swore in Lyndon Baines Johnson as the thirty-sixth President of the United States. Standing nearby, looking on in total shock, was Jackie, still in her bloody pink suit. Camelot was dead. Who could have anticipated such a sudden and horrible demise! Nor could anyone share the special grief that Jackie bore alone. The hopes they had shared had seemed so certain of fulfillment. And now all of that was as though it had never been. The words from Camelot that JFK had loved so well must have held a special bitterness for Jacqueline as she flew back to Washington with the body of her dead husband:

> In short, there's simply not
> A more convenient spot
> For happy-ever-aftering
> Than here in Camelot.

Early the next morning I received a call informing me that all presidential appointees were requested to pay their final respects to the nation's fallen leader at the White House. A gray rain was falling on that never-to-be-forgotten morning of Saturday, November 23, 1963, as a Department of Justice limousine carried me and my fellow Parole Board members to the front portico of the White House. As we walked up the front steps, all three national television networks had their cameras trained upon us. All invited mourners were being identified as they entered the front door of the White House to pay final tribute to John Fitzgerald Kennedy.

We didn't see any members of the family, who were sharing their private grief with one another. After they had left the Gold Room, where the President's remains were being guarded in a closed coffin draped with a large American flag, the rest of us would follow in order determined by protocol. First to enter the Gold Room after the family had left would be the members of the Supreme Court. Next would come the Cabinet and other presidential appointees, followed by members of Congress. Finally there would be the personal friends who were there by invitation.

As part of that solemn procession, I too walked slowly through the State Dining Room, past the Red Room, past the Blue and the Green Rooms. Conversations were hushed as guarded attempts were made to express the inexpressible, to share unthinkable suspicions, to probe delicately to find what an acquaintance who was perhaps in a better position to know such things might have heard about who Oswald really was and whether there was any hard evidence (as rumor already had it) that Soviet and Cuban intelligence had engineered the assassination. Of course such speculations were not to be aired publicly. So staggering was the nation's grief that, had it been openly suggested that Oswald was an agent of the Soviets and Cubans, President Johnson might not have been able to stifle the cry for war. Time was needed for venting grief and cooling off.

Looking out into the rose garden, I was surprised to see that workmen were already removing the dead President's personal belongings from the Oval Office. I wondered why its new occupant had to personalize that office so quickly . . . or was I witnessing the unfortunate result of mere overzealousness, or perhaps something necessitated by work schedules? But surely in this situation some accommodation could be made in the interest of good taste! Couldn't these unpleasant details have waited until our fallen leader had been laid to rest? I was equally distressed by the careless manner in which the workmen handled items that should have been treated with respect, in memory of the one who had owned, used, and in some cases treasured them. Only a few hours ago he had been the President of the United States! *"The President!"* a protesting voice deep within me shouted angrily. It was particularly disturbing to see the familiar rocking chair parked on a dolly outside, unprotected from the driving rain. It had been such a favorite of Kennedy's.

As we moved slowly toward the Gold Room, I suggested to my good friend, Richard Chappell, "Let's look in on the Green Room." I wanted to spend a few moments remembering President Kennedy as we had last seen him, only three nights before. Chappell nodded mutely. I knew that he felt as I did. Turning aside from the long line of solemn mourners, we stepped into the Green Room together.

In the fireplace, the same wood rested untouched in that unusual arrangement that had so recently caught our attention. The expressions on the faces of Abraham Lincoln and Woodrow Wilson staring so solemnly from their ornate frames were also unchanged. The exquisite furnishings were still in the same precise positions. All the opulent symbols of power remained in place, without a hint that there had been a transfer of leadership. On the surface everything looked the same. Yet the one who had breathed life into these rooms, who had captured the heart of a nation and to some extent the world, was no more.

Here in this room I had pretended to be President

for a few moments; and now the three years of JFK's presidency seemed as brief and unreal as my role-playing. I felt a sudden and staggering insight into the brevity of human life and found myself overwhelmed by the realization that our clothes, furniture, and personal belongings, though so transitory, nevertheless outlast us. He was not yet buried, but already scarcely a trace remained in the White House as evidence that John Fitzgerald Kennedy had resided there for three historic years as President of the United States. Only his favorite rocking chair stood on the sidewalk, abandoned in the rain.

The next several days saw kings, presidents, prime ministers, and other world leaders converge upon Washington to pay final tribute to the memory of the brave young idealist who had become President. As the caisson bearing the slain Commander-in-Chief moved slowly through the streets of Washington, followed by the riderless horse, his widow, family, friends, and national leaders, most of the Western world watched on television, still shocked by unbelief and overwhelming grief.

Had Kennedy been the victim of a deranged assassin, or of a conspiracy, domestic or foreign? That question is still debated today. It seems beyond debate, however, that the assassination of the President—and those of Martin Luther King, Jr., Robert F. Kennedy, and Anwar Sadat, as well as the near-assassinations of President Ronald Reagan and Pope John Paul—are symptoms of a growing moral sickness in society that involves us all. Yet at the same time there is a growing sense of optimism centered in a renewed belief in the inherent goodness of mankind and infinite human potential. The two ideas just don't fit together.

It was a great personal privilege to have been a small

part of the John F. Kennedy Administration. Lois and I shall never forget sharing with the Kennedys in the splendor of Camelot that last night we were all together in the White House. The unthinkable tragedy that overtook them and all of us in Dallas left me in emotional shock at the week's end. It seemed impossible that a warped and unknown man could destroy so quickly and violently the glamour, high excitement, and promise of the New Frontier. Three years of hope and hard work had suddenly been cut off from the present, and all that remained was the memory of "one shining moment" in a twentieth-century legend.

John Fitzgerald Kennedy had eagerly pursued his dream of a peaceful world where might serves right. That dream could not be destroyed by the rifle shots that shattered his body. Dreams live in hearts and minds. Whether that dream will become flesh and bone in a world of genuine peace is the burning question that remains. What will decide this? In his first statement to the nation upon taking office, President Kennedy called us back to a faith that he believed was our only hope for realizing that dream. He did so with these immortal words:

> . . . I have sworn before you and Almighty God the same solemn oath our forebears prescribed nearly a century-and-three-quarters ago.
>
> The world is very different now . . . yet the same revolutionary beliefs for which our forebears fought are still at issue . . . that the rights of man come not from the generosity of the state, but from the hand of God. . . .
>
> With a good conscience our only sure reward, with history the final judge of our deeds, let us go forth . . . asking His blessing and His

help . . . knowing that here on earth God's work
must truly be our own.

Was this just rhetoric designed to appeal to that mass
of voters still naive enough to believe in and depend upon
a God from whom modern technology had emancipated
us? Or did this great man really believe what he said? How
dared a President in his inaugural address imply that the
only hope for the world was for governments themselves
to acknowledge that justice, peace, and equality came
only through obedience to God! Wasn't this appeal a violation of the "separation of church and state"? What
would happen to this nation if we seriously began to
practice JFK's exhortation that our purpose in life was
to do the work of God?

In my own life as a criminologist, I had been confronted
daily by such questions. The assassination of President
Kennedy was a horrible crime, but it was only one murder
among thousands. And Oswald was only one criminal
among hundreds of thousands. As a member and Chairman of the Federal Parole Board, I had faced some of the
most infamous criminals of this century. Could our nation
afford to ignore any longer the lessons and challenges
that their lives and deaths have brought to us? If faced
in the context of the belief that John F. Kennedy declared
to be the great issue in the world today, this challenge
could bring hope instead of despair.

2

Birdman in a Cage

A bird hasteth to the snare, and knoweth not
that it is for his life.

It was a dark and bitter March morning in 1958,
unusually so even for San Francisco. While the city slept,
a thick and penetrating fog had crept stealthily up from
the Bay. The persistent monotony of foghorns that had
troubled my sleep throbbed in eerie warning blasts
through the murk. Leaving the warmth of the hotel lobby,
I pulled my overcoat closer about me and headed for the
waiting car that the warden of Alcatraz had sent for me.

"Good morning, Judge Reed!" The greeting was almost
swallowed up in the swirling fog as my driver leaped out
to open the door.

"Good morning, Fred!" I eased into the backseat with
my briefcase beside me, and in a moment we were on
our way toward the nearby Bay.

"Funny how we always say *good* morning no matter

29

what," he remarked wryly. "It's a mighty cold one today!"

"And gloomy . . . even for this town!" I added, peering out at the heavy traffic that seemed to materialize mysteriously out of the gray mist, only to vanish as suddenly. On either side of the street the undefined shapes of office buildings appeared and disappeared in the same fantasy parade.

"I'll have you down to the launch in no time," the driver called back reassuringly. "I can see right through this stuff . . . I'm used to it."

Skillfully he wound his way through the impossible traffic and down the frighteningly steep hills of San Francisco toward the docks. Gradually I relaxed and settled back into the seat. The fog had only temporarily taken my mind from the business that lay before me. Now my thoughts returned to the heavy caseload of parole hearings I faced that day inside the thick walls of Alcatraz, known not so affectionately as The Rock.

"This is Your day, Lord," I prayed. "It's in Your hands. Please guide me. . . ." I had proved over many years of private life and public service that God would indeed keep me in His will, even in Washington D.C., if I really wanted Him to—and I did.

As Chairman of the Federal Parole Board, I was very conscious of the many problems plaguing both the federal and state prison systems. The overcrowded conditions fostered violence among inmates, increasing the likelihood that guards would overreact. Pressure was being exerted by the proponents of two opposing philosophies: on one side the clamor to build more prisons and on the other side the pleas to cut down on imprisonment, substituting more constructive methods of punishment for nonviolent offenders. There was the criticism of judges who, for lack of adequate facilities, tended to

leniency, even when serious crimes were involved. And then there was the matter of parole. Some critics leveled scathing broadsides against parole boards for being unfeeling and hard; others complained bitterly that dangerous criminals were being turned back into the streets to prey once again upon society.

There were more than enough administrative duties to take up all my time in Washington. However, I tried to take my turn as often as possible at hearing individual cases firsthand inside the many federal penitentiaries across the country. I considered it important to get a feel for what was going on in the prisons through these personal visits. Touring the facilities, I talked with the wardens and guards, met with the prisoners in their cells and workshops, asked questions, took notes, and asked more questions.

"I heard that one of those guys applying for parole threatened to kill you last time, Judge." The words resurrected a painful memory. "Right in front of witnesses, too!" he added. "He must have been crazy. They get that way."

"He was serving three life sentences; after all, nothing could make it any worse for him," I replied, remembering very vividly the incident and the compassion I had felt, in spite of his threat, for this haunted man. Behind the hatred in his eyes I had sensed a hopeless despair. Life that once had held the promise of joy and childhood dreams fulfilled was slipping away in a stream of tedious days spent caged like an animal. He had lashed out at me because I represented what he called "the system" that held him its prisoner. He couldn't possibly understand that the love and forgiveness which I, though a member of that hated establishment, felt for him were genuine. Yet it was true, and only because I had tasted Christ's love and forgiveness in my own life.

Ever since my appointment to the Federal Parole Board
in 1953, and especially since becoming its Chairman four
years later, I had felt very acutely the heavy responsibility
of deciding the fate of the many thousands of men under
its jurisdiction. My own experience had confirmed the
wisdom of what the Bible teaches: that the exercise of
authority by some men over others was absolutely essential for the preservation of human life and safety; but
without God to set the standard, there could be no justice. I knew from my years in government that power
had a strange, almost irresistible way of corrupting
people, and that those who were not conscious of God's
authority over them and were not submissive to His will
often abused the power entrusted to them. Long, bitter
years spent in federal prisons, blaming everyone but
themselves, often gave inmates an acute sensitivity to
such abuse—which they then pointed to as justification
for their criminal behavior. Only as I myself was subject
to God's authority could I act wisely and fairly in
exercising the grave responsibility entrusted to me.

"You'd better be extra careful today!" The driver's
concerned voice broke into my thoughts once again.

"Is that right?"

"Yes, Sir! Isn't the 'Birdman' appealing for parole
again?" There was no mistaking the awe in his voice as
he mentioned this special prisoner.

I needed no reminder. The very name of Robert Stroud,
the most famous inmate on The Rock at that time, exuded
a special mystique. Although a convicted murderer, he
was almost worshiped by a cult of admirers around the
world. Whenever Stroud's turn came for a hearing, letters
of appeal poured in like a flood and required a special
staff to answer them. This time had been no exception,
and the reasons given for paroling him were as irrelevant
as ever. For most, his inordinate love for birds was proof

of redemptive kindness if not of outright innocence.

In large part, the peculiar charisma that had attached itself to Robert Stroud was due to a bestseller written about him titled *The Birdman of Alcatraz*. A copy had been sent to me some months before by my good friends Dr. Frank and Rachel Ellis. I had known the author, Thomas E. Gaddis, when we had both served as deputy probation officers for Los Angeles County. Because of my high regard for both Gaddis and the Ellises, I had read the book with great interest. The portrait he drew of Robert Stroud was a captivating one and was painted with unusual skill. There was, however, a good deal of romanticism mixed with fact in the very readable text, and Stroud pretty nearly came off as the hero and society as the villain.

Stroud's life had been an unhappy one from the very beginning, and Gaddis was applying textbook psychology, which rarely explains real life. With an abusive father and an overprotective mother, his was in many ways the classic case of a boy almost destined to run afoul of the law. Although countless others have survived a similar or worse combination of aggravating circumstances, there can be no question that Stroud's life was one long series of unfortunate events that seemed to drive him relentlessly into the arms of the law.

Right from the start, the marriage of Robert's parents, Ben and Elizabeth Stroud, had been doomed by constant friction and growing conflict. Habitually beaten by her first husband, Elizabeth, a proud and attractive woman, had left him and had soon taken up with Ben Stroud. They moved together to Seattle during the summer of 1889, only to discover that it had been almost completely destroyed by fire a few days before their arrival.

Ben found employment and a tent for temporary shelter, and here Elizabeth spent the first months of an uncomfortable pregnancy cooking over an open fire. By the time Robert was born, in January of 1890, they had moved into a small wooden house. Unhappy, however, with the complications and responsibilities forced upon him by a growing family, Ben began to drink heavily. At first he merely ignored his unwanted son. Later he grew progressively more abusive. Young Robert endured frequent and senseless beatings. Often in his drunken frenzy Ben threatened to kill not only this young intruder but his mother as well.

In her heartbroken love for her beloved "Robbie," Elizabeth became paranoid in her protection, not only shielding him from his drunkard father but from a normal life with neighborhood children as well. When he should have been out playing with the other boys, "Robbie" was kept inside for lessons in American history and told repeatedly what a bright and special person he was. Elizabeth proudly developed young Robert's intellectual inclinations, hoping to ensure for him a higher station in life than his father had, and one more in keeping with that of her own family.

In those early years, his mother's obsessive control over Robert afforded the only refuge from his father's hostility. It also robbed him, however, of the experiences he needed in the give-and-take of growing up with other children his own age. Soon he was being shunned as peculiar. The marked favoritism that his father showed toward his younger brother Marcus had a further debilitating effect. When in 1898 Ben Stroud joined the hordes of fortune-seekers that stampeded to the Yukon, young Robert's inner turmoil was accentuated by the uncertainties of life in this wild and lawless new frontier.

Shunned by his contemporaries, and chafing at last under the restraints of his mother's constant attention and protection, young Robert began hanging around the docks. For a 12-year-old it was quite an education. Near his thirteenth birthday, Robert's parents' strained and long-doomed relationship finally exploded in a violent quarrel over Ben's affair with another woman. Elizabeth told him to move in with his girlfriend, which he promptly did, returning only to bring money occasionally and to see Marc, his favored younger son.

Robert did the predictable: He ran away, leaving a note to tell his mother that he loved her. For two turbulent years he rode the rails and lived with the flotsam and jetsam of transient society, while crisscrossing the country in search of some identity and purpose. Dissatisfied with that life at last and apparently repentant, he returned home, found a job, and turned most of his earnings over to his mother.

Robert's restlessness, however, and periodic encounters with his father drove him away again, this time to seek his fortune in the roaring boomtown of Cardova, Alaska. There young Robert, now 18, began to follow in the footsteps of the father he hated. He moved in with his first woman, a dance-hall girl named Kitty O'Brien. They soon drifted on to Juneau, where Kitty found work in a cabaret and Stroud, unemployed, grew more morose in the idleness of the long, dark winter. Events rushed to a climax. Gaddis told the tale in far more readable and interesting style than the official records that I had left in the files in Washington, D.C.:

> On January 18, 1909 . . . [when] young Stroud returned to the room he and Kitty shared, he found Kitty groaning on the bed. Both her eyes were blackened and there was a red line on her neck. Her locket was missing. Stroud poured her a strong drink of whiskey.
>
> "Kill the beast, kill him, kill him!" she whimpered.

Stroud bathed her bruises and plied her with whiskey.

"Was it Charlie?"

She nodded. "He took my locket with my daughter's picture. Said he's keeping it until I come to stay with him . . ."

At six-thirty, Charlie Dahmer returned to his cottage and fumbled in the dark. He struck a match and lit his lamp. The light fell upon Stroud sitting in one corner with his hat on. He stood, the lamplight flickering against his long, lean face. He watched Charlie, his smile fading.

"Did you beat Kitty?" Stroud's long arm hung loose. His heavy overcoat swung open.

Charlie stared at the thin youth with the pale face and absurd white Stetson. Charlie's eyes were measuring off the distance from the oilcloth-covered table to the corner . . .

Suddenly he lunged, head down, arms outstretched like a tackler. Stroud's left hand dug into his belt. He got the gun out quickly. He fired and missed. Charlie bore down on him. Stroud fired again, pointblank. Charlie came on. Stroud slammed the gun against his head. The bartender crashed to the floor at Stroud's feet, one outstretched arm twitching on the rung of the chair.

Charlie was dead after the second shot. The autopsy showed the bullet entering high on the right temple and following a line down to his pelvis.*

These then were the basic facts which surrounded the

---

* Thomas E. Gaddis, *Birdman of Alcatraz* (Aeonian Press, 1955), pp. 18-19.

man and his original crime. Today I would have to take a hard look at the years since prison doors had slammed behind him and make a decision about his future.

Arriving at the docks, I sensed a tension among my fellow commuters to The Rock as I climbed aboard the *James V. Bennett* launch. These were all hard-bitten prison personnel, who generally endured their job of guarding dangerous criminals with an air of long-suffering boredom. But today something unusual was in the air. One of them approached me, holding out a cup of steaming coffee.

"Good morning, Judge Reed! Care for some coffee?"

"Good morning, even if it isn't," I replied, taking the proffered coffee gratefully. "Looks like good brew. Thanks. You sure need something hot on a morning like this!" There was something else on the man's mind. He edged a bit closer.

"This is a big day for Alcatraz, Judge!" he ventured. I was surprised at the almost childish excitement in his voice.

"A big day?" I asked, genuinely puzzled. "What do you mean?"

"Stroud's on the docket today, isn't he?"

I nodded. "What's so special about that?"

"Well, the scuttlebutt on The Rock is . . . that not only will Stroud's case be heard today . . . but the Parole Board is going to release him!" He looked importantly around at the tight group of listeners.

So that was the reason for all the excitement! I felt a dozen pairs of eyes scrutinizing me closely for any change in expression that would confirm the rumor.

I smiled and shook my head. "You ought to know better than that. These things aren't decided ahead of time. We haven't had the hearing yet . . . and it takes a majority vote of the Board after all the facts are in . . . ."

My attempted explanation was cut short by the clanging of the ship's bell and several sharp blasts on the shrill whistle. I felt a lurch as the launch pulled away from the dock to begin its brief cruise across the rough waters of San Francisco Bay. As we moved out beyond the shelter of the shore, the cold wind stiffened, blowing foam from the mounting whitecaps across the deck and into our faces. Once again I felt the sense of awe, almost fear, that gripped me on each trip I made to this isolated, escape-proof prison.

The small, forbidding island of solid rock, discovered by the Spaniards in 1796 and named after the pelicans (alcatraces) that covered it in those early days, had not become a United States possession until 1851. Its first use had been as a fortification. Then in 1868 the beginnings of a prison had been constructed there, to be used at first to confine rebellious Indian leaders and disciplinary cases among the military. Later, in 1933, it would be taken over by the Federal Bureau of Prisons to meet the need for an escape-proof facility to which the worst inmates could be transferred from other federal prisons.

Alcatraz was feared by inmates of other institutions. Hardened men had been known to plead not to be sent there. Twenty-six escape attempts had all failed. Though five bodies had never been recovered, it was doubtful that any of them had survived the treacherous currents that swept on all sides of The Rock. The only possible exceptions could have been Ralph Roe and "Sunny Boy" Cole in 1937. If indeed they did make it through those deadly waters alive, their stolen cache of 200,000 dollars would have made it possible for them to drop out of sight and into anonymity.

Looming out of the mist, The Rock took dim shape at last. Stained dark by the perpetual dew, fog, and rain, the thick walls of the fortress seemed an extension of the rock island itself. Forbidding enough from the outside, within it was a maze of steel barricades, confining bars, automatic locks, electric eyes, tall guard towers, and catwalks—even teargas bombs suspended from the ceiling over the tables in the dining room. A "hell hole" is what one former Attorney General, Frank Murphy, had aptly called it.

Even I was not immune to security clearance, which included an I.D. check, a number branded on the back of my hand, and a series of electronic body scans. Only then was I permitted on the bus, which proceeded slowly up the narrow switchbacks on the one-way road winding back and forth up the precipitous climb to the front gate of the prison.

Just on the other side of the access road was the back door of the Warden's house, no more than a stone's throw from the private entrance that gave him easy admittance to the administrative section of the prison complex. The spacious, well-appointed residence had been built on a jutting ledge of rock with a southern exposure. Its wide living room window looked out on the most fantastic view imaginable of the Bay, the skyline of San Francisco, and the Golden Gate Bridge beyond.

That breathtaking view had been capitalized upon more than once. When important appropriations for Alcatraz were needed, members of the Budget Committee would be flown out to tour the prison. Such visits were always highlighted by a gourmet dinner for the dignitaries from San Francisco and Washington D.C. The unobstructed panorama, if the night was clear, was absolutely unforgettable. A million lights blazed across the seven hills of San Francisco and down to the water's edge, decorating the otherwise-drab docks. To the west, suspended above the black void of water and marking the entrance to the Bay, more lights were strung like glittering diamond necklaces from the towers of the Golden Gate Bridge.

A security officer led me through three interlocking steel gates into the administration area. Warden Paul Madigan, who had come to Alcatraz from Minnesota, was waiting for me in his office. Sharing a number of mutual friends and experiences, we had developed a great deal of respect and warmth for each other through our years of friendship.

"It's good to see you again, George!" he exclaimed, extending his hand. "Mrs. Madigan and I are expecting you to join us for lunch as usual."

"I'm looking forward to that," I replied gratefully. "You haven't lost the view, have you?"

"It comes and goes," he said philosophically. "If the fog lifts by noon. . . ." He shrugged and left the words hanging.

"Judge Reed!"

I turned to see the Chief Security Officer standing in the doorway. "At your convenience, Sir, the first case, Robert Stroud, Alcatraz number 17431, is ready to be heard on his application for parole."

"All security precautions have been taken," the Warden assured me as I picked up my briefcase and turned to leave his office. "Have a good morning!" he added cheerfully.

A few steps brought me to the hearing room. As I awaited Stroud's arrival I mentally reviewed the salient facts of the case which were already so familiar to me and to the public.

After his conviction for the murder of Charlie Dahmer, on August 23, 1909, Robert Stroud had been sentenced by a federal judge to the statutory limit: 12 years in the McNeil Island Federal Penitentiary. Similar to Alcatraz but larger, it was also a bird refuge and had a fabulous view of Mount Rainier. McNeil was also an island fortress, separated from the nearest shore by 12 miles of water. Its warden, O.P. Holligans, was a tough disciplinarian. Unwilling to bow to any authority, even if it would earn him an earlier release for good behavior, Stroud refused from the very beginning to fit into the prison "system." He hated the administration and staff and was violently independent in his dealings with other prisoners. In his last fight at McNeil, Stroud buried a paring knife in the shoulder of another inmate, whom he accused of "snitching" on him.

Because of his habitually hostile attitude and violent behavior, Stroud was shipped with 50 other dangerous inmates to a new maximum-security section of Leavenworth Federal Prison in Kansas. There he enrolled in a special school run by the University of Kansas inside the prison. Reverting back to the early academic training of his mother, "Robbie" studied mathematics, astronomy, and structural engineering, earning good grades in each subject. Motivated by a burning hatred of what he called "Christian bigots," he also studied Eastern mysticism and occultism. Attracted to the possibility of developing supernatural "mind power," he dabbled in reincarnation, karma, and telepathy. Hinduism had a peculiar appeal to Stroud because of its denial of the reality of sin, its rejection of moral absolutes, and its teaching that each person's "dharma" (way of life) must be individually determined.

At last Robert Stroud had found a religion that justified his hatred of authority. No one had the right to impose any standards upon him. What he had done to Charlie Dahmer was not murder at all, but the inevitable result of the karma (the "law of cause and effect") that each of them had built up in prior lives. Charlie had it coming to him. The real crime was committed by those who had imprisoned him for giving Charlie what he deserved. The inexorable law of karma would eventually exact its payment from each of those bigots—and he would play whatever part he could in that vengeance! Stroud began to use the unique skills he had acquired in the structural engineering course to produce distinctive and efficient weapons. With consummate skill, he transformed stolen kitchen knives into miniature Roman swords with razor-sharp parallel edges and short leather handles. These he passed along to his friends to help them work out their own karma.

In the crowded prison dining hall on Sunday, March 16, 1916, Robert Stroud held up his hand in the designated signal of illness or personal need. A guard named Turner, whom Stroud hated with a passion, motioned for him to approach to explain his problem. They met face-to-face in an aisle. Turner was apparently not satisfied with whatever Stroud told him. Their brief exchange of words grew quickly heated. Turner grabbed at his club, but Stroud also got a grip on it. There was a brief struggle. Turner managed to gain sole possession of the heavy stick and seemed to be in control. Stroud stepped back. Then he suddenly reached inside his prison jacket and with one swift motion buried a carefully engineered knife in Turner's chest. As the dying guard dropped his club and collapsed on top of it, a wild-eyed Stroud stood over him, sobbing and cursing, the blood-stained miniature Roman sword still gripped in his hand. Unaware of what had happened, the prison band continued to play "In Paradise." In the prison shakedown that followed, 26 knives similar to Stroud's were discovered in the possession of various prisoners.

It took four days for the jury in a Kansas Federal Court to return a verdict of first-degree murder. On May 27, 1916, Judge John C. Pollock sentenced Robert Stroud to be "hanged by the neck until dead." In a miraculous break for Stroud, the Federal Circuit Court sustained an appeal on the basis of a judicial error and declared a mistrial. On May 28, 1917, after seven hours of deliberation following a second trial, the jury declared, "We find the defendant, Robert F. Stroud, guilty as charged. . . *without capital punishment.*" The judge immediately imposed a life sentence.

Anyone else would have considered himself fortunate to have escaped execution. Not Robert Stroud. His hatred of all authority seemed to blind him to the obvious. Or was he convinced that his karma held something even better for him? Against the advice of his court-appointed attorney, Stroud insisted upon an appeal, which resulted in the United States Supreme Court ordering yet another trial in August 1917. On June 28, 1918, the third jury declared Stroud "guilty as charged," and the judge, as his lawyers had warned, sentenced him to be hanged inside Leavenworth on Friday, November 8, 1918. More legal maneuvers all the way to the Supreme Court again succeeded only in postponing the date of execution to April 23, 1920.

Through it all, Stroud's mother and his brother Marc remained faithful to their beloved "Robbie." Elizabeth Stroud expended herself in desperate appeals to Washington officials, begging for the life of her son. Senator J. Hamilton Lewis of Illinois was so moved by her tears that he took her to see the wife of President Woodrow Wilson. Compelled by the stubborn loyalty of a mother's love, the First Lady carried the passionate request along with the official papers to the ailing President. As a result of his grief over the failure of the Senate to confirm United States participation in the League of Nations, Wilson had suffered a stroke that would eventually take his life. For months his wife had sheltered him from public contact and had assumed total responsibility for the presidency herself. Whatever transpired between them on this fateful day, and for whatever reasons, when Edith Bowling Wilson returned the papers to Elizabeth Stroud, there, across the face of the execution order, in Wilson's faltering scrawl, were the precious words: "Commuted to life. W. W."

This then was the man who would in a moment appear before me. He had cheated death in 1920, just eight days before his scheduled hanging. Would he win the rest today—his freedom? Two months earlier he had turned 68. Nearly 50 of those hapless years had been passed in federal prisons. Could I deny him that breath of freedom in the last few years of his life? Hadn't he more than paid his debt to society? What possible purpose could further incarceration serve? My own thoughts wavered and echoed momentarily the arguments repeated so persuasively in the flood of letters that still poured in on behalf of the "Birdman."

"Prisoner number 17431!" With that loud announcement, Robert Stroud was led in with military precision and seated about 20 feet directly in front of me. One huge, muscular, and specially trained security guard stationed himself on either side of the prisoner. Though he wasn't a large man, Stroud was wiry and was known to move like a cat.

"This is a rehearing of your case before the Federal Parole Board," I informed Prisoner number 17431, "scheduled in keeping with Board policy, which provides that all Federal prisoners shall be heard at least semiannually, in spite of the nature or length of their sentences. Do you have anything to add to your written statement?"

"First, I'd like to ask about Warden Johnston," countered Stroud in a surprise move. The tone was conciliatory and friendly. "Is he keeping well?" James "Saltwater" Johnston had been in charge of Alcatraz when Stroud had arrived there from Leavenworth. We had been very close friends.

"I'm sorry to say that Warden Johnston is dead." I wondered whether Stroud had really not heard the news, or was just putting on an act.

Stroud appeared to be genuinely shocked. "I'm distressed to learn of his death. . . he was a good man!"

Earning the reputation of a tough but fair warden at Alcatraz, Johnston had succeeded where others had failed in gaining at least a measure of cooperation from Stroud. Johnston had moved on to the Federal Parole Board in Washington D.C. We had been sworn in together in 1953, ten years after Stroud had been transferred to Alcatraz. Though other men might plead, "Anywhere but The Rock!" Stroud would never have allowed himself to beg from any authority figure. Still, his demeanor had undergone, for this occasion at least, a radical change for the better.

"He was a good man, Warden Johnston," repeated Stroud with what sounded like real feeling in his voice. It was the nearest to anything sentimental I had heard from him. "A good man. I never had any quarrel with him."

"I'm glad to hear that," I replied cordially. I had seven hearings scheduled for that day, but this kind of friendly exchange was excellent—within limits. "Warden Johnston and I often had lunch together and talked about his years here at Alcatraz," I added. We had also talked about Stroud, but that was confidential. Johnston had warned me that number 17431 could be a *very* dangerous man— especially when challenged by authority.

Stroud had good reason to remember Johnston with fondness. On more than one occasion, the former warden had told me that he had tried to make life at Alcatraz as bearable as he could for every prisoner, including

Stroud. In spite of Stroud's bad record at other federal prisons, Johnston had allowed him four hours of outdoor exercise per week and other "first-class" privileges. It was tough, no-nonsense "Saltwater" Johnston who had made it possible for the publication, late in 1943, of *Stroud's Digest of the Diseases of Birds.*

Years before, at Leavenworth, after President Wilson had rescued him from the gallows, Stroud had developed his first interest in birds and their diseases. It began with the gift of a pair of canaries from a fellow prisoner. The birds mated, the eggs hatched, and Stroud was on his way to worldwide fame. As his canaries multiplied, so did their diseases. Observing carefully and patiently, Stroud experimented and recorded in meticulously detailed notes. He added constantly to his growing fund of knowledge, which he refined and expanded further through correspondence with bird fanciers far and wide. These people in turn began to spread the word about this amazing prisoner, who seemed to know "everything about canaries." Soon newspapers were carrying the story, and Stroud's reputation as an expert on birds grew with each new article.

It was, however, a bureaucratic ruling out of Washington D.C. that made Robert Stroud almost a household word. In July 1931, the Federal Bureau of Prisons notified Warden White that Robert Stroud must dispose of his birds. The story was carried by newspapers across the country, and radio commentators such as Lowell Thomas announced the news over national networks. A storm of protest quickly grew to hurricane proportions among bird-lovers around the world. The President of the United States and members of Congress were deluged by thousands of letters decrying the order separating Stroud from his birds. More than 50,000 signatures were gathered on petitions circulated by bird clubs and sent to the President.

In the face of such pressure, the federal bureaucracy backed down and Stroud's birds were returned to him. Overnight Stroud had become a hero with a following that carried weight in the nation's capital. Elated by that victory, he worked day and night to prove to the world that he was worthy of all those letters and petitions. In a marathon feat of almost nonstop writing, Stroud completed a 60,000-word manuscript on canary diseases in 60 days. This would have been a herculean achievement for even the most accomplished writer, considering the highly technical nature of the subject. Somehow Stroud had the treatise smuggled out of Leavenworth. The critics hailed it as the first scientific treatise to classify in detail the diseases of canaries.

Being a celebrity made Stroud even more contemptuous of authority. He became almost impossible to handle, clashing openly with Warden Walter A. Hunter at every opportunity. The final straw for Hunter was the discovery of yet another manuscript, this one highly critical of the Leavenworth administration and staff, including Hunter himself and the Director of Federal Prisons. To teach the "Birdman" a lesson, the Warden promptly confiscated the offending manuscript as well as Stroud's radio and bird supplies. With royalties coming in, Stroud hired an attorney, who filed a writ against Hunter for unwarranted persecution. That case was pending when Stroud was transferred to Alcatraz, where his fame continued to grow under the watchful encouragement of Warden Johnston.

Here, in a large cell specially constructed for Stroud, and with a magnificent view of the Bay, he wrote a new treatise. *Stroud's Digest of the Diseases of Birds* quickly became a sensational success and further enhanced his reputation as a leading authority on the diagnosis and treatment of bird diseases. Glowing reviews were written, two of them by university professors.

Having exhausted the subject of former Warden John-ston, Stroud launched into his appeal. He had studied law at Alcatraz and spoke eloquently and knowledgeably, albeit with an almost professional air of restraint. "Many universities consider my work to be the very best on the subject," he reminded me softly, with a pretense of humility that was completely out of character. Then he looked me in the eye and added with a more character-istic tone: "I think I've proved myself during almost 17 years right here in Alcatraz."

I didn't tell him that his former warden had never yet cast a vote in favor of paroling him, nor had anyone else on the Board that I could remember. Surely he knew how dangerous Johnston himself had considered him to be. Did he think he was convincing me? He was speaking in carefully chosen words, and his tall, thin frame was weaving back and forth in cadence with his low-pitched, deliberately hypnotic tone of voice. His interest in the occult had taken Stroud into the study of hypnosis. The file contained reports by clinical psychologists and other Board members of his attempts to exercise a hypnotic influence over authorities.

I held up my hand and interrupted him. "I know what you're trying to do," I said bluntly. "Weaving back and forth like a pendulum. . . ."

Continuing to sway, but now only slightly, he looked at me with large unblinking eyes in an attempt to effect an air of childish innocence. "What do you mean?"

"I'm well aware of your attempts to practice hypno-sis. It's not going to work this morning. . . it doesn't impress or affect me at all. This is your hearing, and you can make it whatever you want. . . it's your record, but I'd suggest that you stop trying to play that game."

The swaying stopped immediately. His eyes hardened almost imperceptibly.

"You had a recent conference with one of the most famous psychiatrists in the world," I reminded him. "How did it go?"

"We got along."

"Nothing more to report than that?"

"He didn't help me . . . and he didn't tell me anything new. It's the same old horse under a different blanket. They all say the same monotonous thing. Right out of the textbooks."

"Anything more you want to add?"

"I just don't understand what else I can do to prove my value to society. I've done more good than most people living outside. What more do you want?"

The report of a world-renowned psychiatrist had indicated that Robert Stroud was still an extremely dangerous man. Years of imprisonment had effected no fundamental change in his basic outlook on life. He was an absolute individualist, determined to live by his own impulses and prone to violence when challenged. His individuality meant even more to him than freedom. It was a tragedy for a human being to be locked away under tight security and close scrutiny for 50 years and to know that he would be there until he died. I felt sorry for him. Yet I knew that he had shown not the slightest inclination to adjust his attitude toward the rest of humanity and that he would be a danger to society if the Board succumbed to its natural sympathy and released him.

Robert F. Stroud, Alcatraz #17431, was indeed a "birdman in a cage," a prisoner of his own making. Perhaps he had grown so attached to his specially made VIP cell that he really didn't want to leave. Was that why he persisted in a battle of wills that he couldn't possibly win?

Apparently Stroud could only find happiness in bending the rest of the world to his iron will. So insightful in other ways, in this area of life he seemed blind. A bitter, unhappy man, Stroud stubbornly refused to admit his personal guilt. Not for him the catharsis of repentance and renewal.

Stroud had the capability of accomplishing almost anything. Within ten years after arriving at Alcatraz, he had consumed every English volume in the entire prison library. So, with the aid of a dictionary, he started on the French classics in the library. It was slow, painful going, but he had plenty of time. Soon he was reading them through laboriously, but with growing proficiency and understanding. Sharing his love of French literature in a letter to Fred Dow, an 80-year-old bird fancier who had corresponded with him for 26 years, Stroud opened the window of his soul a rare crack:

> We have known each other a long time, Fred. We have always gotten along well, which just goes to show that we are not such old cranks as some people would make us out to be.
>
> I wish you could read French, Fred. I would have you read "Le Voyage" from *Les Fleurs du Mal*, by Charles Baudelaire. This fellow was very bitter at life, and he had reason to be, but it was that very bitterness of life that made him one of the greatest poets who ever lived. I have a bunch of his poems that I have copied and am learning by heart. In the one mentioned, he says in one verse:
>
> > It is bitter to know what one learns
> > from travel;
> > that the world is small and monotonous;

that yesterday, today, tomorrow and
   forever,
it makes us see our own image;
an oasis of horror in a desert of ennui.

Was Stroud revealing to Fred Dow the secret source
of his own inspiration? Was it his bitterness that gave him
the determination to prove to himself and society that
he could turn bird-watching into a science? Would the
world have missed the benefits of that peculiar genius
if he had never gone to prison? Or would that genius have
blossomed and flowered even more fully, though perhaps in different ways, had he remained a free man? What
does it mean to be "free"? Is anyone free, or are we all
prisoners unaware? Is the only way to genuine freedom
to become the "prisoners" of God through surrendering
our lives into His hands?

Life so often weaves strange patterns that seem to
involve more than mere chance. Trying to explain the
inexplicable, poets have called us all the prisoners of
"fate." But what is "fate"? And what of the choices we
all make? Stroud chose to believe in "karma" because it
absolved him of moral responsibility for his choices and
deeds: He wasn't a criminal—his victims had it coming
to them. Unfortunately, that Eastern philosophy allows
no forgiveness. Stroud would himself have to suffer the
same deaths in future lives that he had meted out to
others. Supposedly *this* would pay his karmic debt; yet
in the process it would perpetuate the very crimes he was
paying for. Those who in turn did him in would themselves have to become similar victims to pay their "karmic
debt". . . .and thus an endless chain of sin and suffering
would be perpetuated, with no possible solution.

There is really no way that any human being can pay
for his own sins. Repentance and forgiveness and a new

life are the only hope, but this seems to involve a miracle in the heart that courts, prisons, group therapy, and rehabilitation programs, no matter how sophisticated or well-intentioned, are in themselves helpless to produce.

Men like Stroud were a burden of concern that I carried for 23 years in Washington D.C. under five presidents. In my heart there were so many prisoners I wanted to see freed. In some cases, however, such well-intentioned compassion would have violated my oath obligating me to the millions of people who were trusting the courts and prisons and parole boards to protect them from known criminals. Nor would it always have been fair to the prisoners themselves. For some, the temptations they would have confronted in freedom could have led to even greater tragedy than they had already brought upon themselves and others. Even though most of us prefer not to believe it, some men *are* so dangerous that prisons are necessary. The challenge of administering justice in a manner that was fair to both society and the criminal was at times overwhelming.

We had plenty of critics who told the Federal Parole Board how to handle criminals. One of the most famous was Burt Lancaster. His letter of invitation* to a special Washington D.C. screening of *Birdman of Alcatraz*, in which he starred, reflected his bias and his intent. I accepted. When we met afterwards, I commented to the effect that had I gone by the script of the movie I, too, would have favored Stroud's release. I'm sure my meaning was not lost on Mr. Lancaster.

Many of those who took up Stoud's cause believed that "freedom" was the cure-all. Others insisted that all humans are inherently good and that this goodness will

---

* For a copy of the letter see Appendix A.

prove itself if only "given a chance." There were psychiatrists who would declare the accused insane, allowing him to escape the consequences of his crime, then after a short while in an asylum conveniently declare him sane again.

In this way, many pathological criminals have been turned loose to prey upon more victims. The diagnoses that psychiatric "experts" have supplied the courts have, unfortunately, subsequently proven to be wrong more often than right. The diagnoses given by different psychiatrists are often so diverse that one finds it hard to believe they are talking about the same case! There are sociologists and criminologists representing differing schools of thought on the subject of crime, punishment, and rehabilitation. It is a complex problem with no easy solution. Yet we members of the Federal Parole Board had to decide the fate of tens of thousands of human beings. And we had to live with our decisions and their consequences year after year.

Robert F. Stroud, The Birdman of Alcatraz, was never paroled. His admirers by the thousands pressured and criticized us for not freeing him. To many bird-lovers, Stroud's work with birds was proof enough that he was basically a "good person" who ought to be "given a chance." We wanted to believe it too, and we wanted to give him that chance—but he was willing to take it only on his own terms. We had evidence that we had to take into account which was unknown to his fans. There were years of hard experience and study behind those difficult decisions. We were criminologists who studied criminals as closely as Stroud studied birds.

But we were also human beings, and we felt very deeply the pain and disappointment that our decisions produced every day. It often seemed difficult for our critics to view us as human, with deep and responsive feelings of our own. On the other hand, I sometimes found it difficult to see myself as Chairman of the Federal Parole Board, a professional criminologist. I certainly had not intended or even imagined such a career while growing up on the family ranch in Nebraska.

3

Train Up a Child

Train up a child in the way he should go, and
when he is old he will not depart from it.

The Reed Ranch, with its 600 head of black Angus cattle
and assorted horses, hogs, and dairy cows, sprawled over
2000 rolling acres in Dundy County, Nebraska. It was
18 miles to Haigler, the nearest town. With a population
of about 500 in the early 1900's, that tiny community
of neat frame houses on dirt streets boasted its own
physician. Its short main street, lined with gaudily painted
storefronts, served as commercial center for the scattered
ranchers and farmers in the surrounding territory. In
the summer, huge horse-drawn wagons loaded with hay
and grain choked Haigler's one dusty thoroughfare. The
drivers would spend time in shopping, drinking, and
exchanging the latest gossip before returning home with
groceries and supplies and the heavy black coal that was
stockpiled in basements to heat the isolated ranch houses
throughout the long, severe winter.

The Reeds made the coal stretch farther by burning with it corncobs and pasture chips. The latter gave off a surprisingly pleasant and delicate aroma. Some of my earliest memories were centered around the huge pot-bellied stove that radiated its comforting warmth from the center of the huge kitchen/dining room of our Nebraska farm home. On Saturday nights the huge wash-tub was brought into that same room and filled with hot water. Bath time was almost like a purification ceremony in preparation for church the next morning. Cleanliness and godliness were somehow related. Beginning with the youngest, each child was scrubbed until his skin tingled and glowed. That high state of cleanliness was expected to last all day Sunday.

"Cleo! I knew it! You've got another boy!" The excited announcement of my birth came from jolly, gregarious neighbor and close friend Mrs. Frank Strowbridge, who assisted my mother with the delivery at 6:30 A.M. on May 31, 1914. Arriving from Haigler in his fancy buggy two hours later, Dr. Priemer officially pronounced me a healthy specimen.

"We knew his lungs and voice were in top shape," Mother responded, already forgetting her disappointment that she hadn't gotten the little girl she had been hoping for. My father, Edwin W. Reed, and my two older brothers, Harold William and Edwin Paul, were glad that another pair of hands would soon be growing callouses along with theirs. There were seemingly endless acres of corn and hay to plant, harvest, store, and dispense to the animals during the winter. The arrival of a fourth son, John Wesley, 13 months later completed the family.

Genuinely respected and loved by all of us in those pre-generation-gap days, Father was the undisputed head of the house. A tender and compassionate man, whose love for each family member was both inspiring and comforting, he could nevertheless be very stern when discipline was required. The wide leather razor strap was never spared when Father was convinced that any of his sons deserved it. Like my mother, he was a hard worker and expected the same diligence from each of us, with no excuses accepted. It never occurred to us to rebel or complain about the rigors of life on the ranch. By training and example, Father developed in his four sons the qualities he possessed and considered essential: reliability, persistence, honesty, and courtesy. Above all, he taught us to fear and love God, but to fear no man. Mother gave her love and warm understanding impartially to each of us. As we grew and matured, her kindly sympathy and support carried us over many of life's obstacles that might otherwise have seemed insurmountable.

Ranch life was tough, but rich with the warmth of genuine personal relationships. Though separated widely by their vast tracts of land, and working long, hard hours, the ranchers had a strong sense of community and were quick to help one another when a need arose. It was unnecessary to lock doors. Crime was almost unknown. Hard work gave us a respect for the fruits of labor, including what others had produced or earned, and left little time for breeding jealousy and personal greed. Confronting raw nature and knowing that our neighbors, though widely scattered, faced the same rigors and were always ready to help, created a sense of intracommunity fellowship. I was very much aware of this as I grew up and began to shoulder my own responsibilities as a vital link in the social fabric.

Bound together through mutual dependence upon each other and the soil, it seemed that everyone knew everyone else. Individual reputations were built and nourished as carefully as any crop or herd. Here was permanence, visibility, accountability. It was no faceless urban mass we had to do with, and concern for reputation was a strong motivation to honesty.

There were some exceptions to the understood code of conduct. On one occasion Father caught red-handed some members of a neighbor's family in the act of stealing some of our cattle. Galloping up on horseback, he kept his rifle trained on them until the small herd had been driven back onto our property and the hole they had cut in the fence had been repaired. Then he sent them on their way with a stern warning of more severe consequences if they ever tried rustling Reed cattle again. Neither asking for nor offering help, and viewed with suspicion by neighbors, this shiftless family kept itself outside the cooperating community. Though never arrested, they provided my first boyish understanding of what it meant to be an "outlaw."

There were eight boys in that family, all older and larger than us four Reeds. They took great delight in ambushing us as we crossed a corner of their property on our way home from the one-room George Washington Reed School. After repeatedly being bested by this superior force, we formed a mutual defense alliance with the Strowbridge boys and Calvin West. Since our opponents were reluctant to trade bullying for a fair fight, their attacks abruptly ceased. Thereafter, constant vigilance was the price of continued peace. It was a further lesson for me that, although might didn't make right, it was often necessary for maintaining it.

I remember being impressed by the fact that our unfriendly neighbors didn't go to church, whereas most of the other ranchers did. It was not that mere church attendance could cure any vice (I never found a church without hypocrites), but a genuine fear of God seemed to produce a deeper honesty of character than mere social pressure. Even as a young boy, I thought I knew why:

You can't fool God, nor can you run away from Him. There is no denying that a firm conviction of God's existence *must* have a salutary influence upon personal behavior. Sins which one might be tempted to commit because no humans would ever know become immediately less inviting when one really believes that God sees and knows all and will bring us to account—here, or in the hereafter, or both.

Father not only believed in God, but claimed to personally know Him. Nor did this seem at all strange to me or my brothers. There was nothing mystical or complicated about this relationship. Father's prayers were not formal or uncertain, but were the sincere heart expression of a man who was speaking with an intimate Friend. His daily life convinced us Reed boys of God's existence long before we had the experience and evidence that eventually persuaded each of us on his own. No matter how hungry we were, no one dared to take a bite at mealtime until Father had thanked God for the food. Orders for the day's work were not issued to us boys or the hired hands until Father had led us all in the morning Bible reading, prayer, and worship. This rugged man was not ashamed to declare his faith in God. I don't recall anyone challenging him or ridiculing his belief. Intellectual arguments would have seemed empty in comparison with his life.

Because Father was so well-known and respected, our home was seldom without visitors. An active leader in both politics and religion, he had helped to found the Nebraska Farmers' Equity Union, the Western Cattleman's Association, and the Western Nebraska Methodist Camp Meeting. He twice ran as a Republican for Congress to represent the Western District of Nebraska in the United States House of Representatives. The second time he came within less than 100 votes of being elected. "The only reason I lost," he loved to explain as he held forth on occasion to a group of visitors, "was because Cleo was praying against me. She didn't want to raise our four sons in Washington D.C., that 'den of iniquity.' "

Mother never denied or apologized for those fervent and apparently effective prayers. We boys knew that our moral character and relationship with our parents meant more to them than political power or prestige. That conviction left a lasting imprint upon our lives.

Travelers passing through always found a warm welcome and a full table at the Reed Ranch. After feeding and quartering their horses in the big barn, we boys would hurry inside, eager to listen to the fascinating tales which the travelers, whether evangelists, salesmen, or politicians, always seemed to bring with them. As summer progressed, the number of ranch hands being fed at the table would steadily grow, augmented by drifters who followed the harvest north. Activity on the ranch reached a fever pitch with the arrival of the oil-burning thrashing machine and its crew, when we all took advantage of the late twilight to get the grain in and stored for winter.

The most regular visitors we had were the circuit-riding Methodist preachers, who came to hold church services for the neighborhood ranchers and their families. Although we were members of the Methodist Church in Haigler, the 18 miles each way limited our attendance there. Instead, we attended Sunday and revival services in the nearby Reed School, named after my grandfather, where a variety of community gatherings and social events were held. There I was deeply affected by many a sobering sermon powerfully delivered by the horseback-riding Methodist preachers, whose obvious sense of mission and urgency was deterred neither by summer rains nor winter

blizzards. I was certain that nothing could stop these messengers of God.

Some of my fondest memories go back to the home-spun Christmas programs in that small country school-house: our childish wonder and excitement, the nervously recited poems and Bible verses, the great relief when lines had been spoken at last with faltering voice. Then followed the laughter and warmth of friends crowded together, the home-baked goodies, and the cold ride home by horse-drawn sleigh across the deep snows. I remember, too, beneath all the fun and celebration and nostalgia of that most special time of the year, my simple pondering over the Christ-child: God becoming a baby in a manger, growing up as a man, and allowing himself to be nailed to a cross in order to die for my sins. Some-how the years rolled by, Christmas and Easter came and went and came again, and still the incarnation and resur-rection remained mysterious, wonderful tales I loved to hear, but whose meaning for me personally remained elusive.

Along with my three brothers, I learned early and repeatedly that life was not a free ride but an ongoing enterprise requiring lots of hard work. Our day began long before the first light of dawn. My bed was so warm and the winter's cold so numbing, but there were cows to milk, livestock to feed, and the barn to clean. I can still smell the familiar odors, hear the early-morning sounds, and feel the packed snow, mud, or hard soil under my feet as I trudged along that well-worn path from house to barn to pens and back. When we headed for the kitchen, there was no dispute as to which flakes to claim at breakfast. We boys dug into ham and eggs and homemade biscuits with honey and plenty of home-canned fruit.

Breakfast and family devotions over, Mom inspected

her four boys, and then it was off to school by horse-back. Woe to those who were not seated behind their desks in time for the lesson to begin! My first teacher, Miss Floy Offin, was an invincible disciplinarian who allowed no nonsense. Justice was meted out with a strict and impartial hand and was backed by the full weight of approval of the School Board and community.

I well remember looking out of the schoolhouse window one never-to-be-forgotten day to see three mounted men, with my father in the lead, galloping into the schoolyard. It was an awesome sight to all of us children, for immediately we recognized them as the official School Board, of which my father was chairman. With grim expressions they marched into the school and seated themselves ominously on the small stage beside the teacher. It seemed like an eternity before my father at last stood to his feet.

"We've received a report," he began in solemn tone, "that three eighth-grade boys have been smoking in the barn!" After a dramatic pause to let that sink in, he continued: "This is not only dangerous to the horses and barn, but to the lungs and health!" It would be decades before that simple wisdom would be acknowledged by the medical profession and the United States government would put its weight behind a campaign to stop smoking —too late to save the lives of many who had thought it manly or sophisticated.

After quoting verbatim the Nebraska Juvenile Court Code forbidding minors to smoke, he added, "Those involved will receive appropriate punishment at home." His eyes seemed to look right into our souls as he concluded: "If this conduct is ever repeated, I will personally see to it that the violators are punished according to the law. And this includes my own four sons!"

My older brother Harold, who would eventually serve 26 years as president of Olivet Nazarene College, got what Father had promised that evening when we returned home. It cured him of smoking and lawbreaking, and the sounds of that leather strap meeting flesh and of Harold's cries cured the rest of us. It also assured us once again that Father really cared about his boys. We never learned who had "snitched."

4

Shaken Foundations

If the foundations be destroyed, what can the righteous do?

The education we received in the one-room George Washington Reed School was heavy on reading, writing, and arithmetic. It was also unabashedly designed to build character. There was a certain God-fearing quality to the instruction that may have been the secret of the low juvenile crime rate in those days. That the rehabilitation of juvenile offenders would one day, in God's plan, bring me to Washington D.C., that very "den of iniquity" that my mother had prayed we children would escape, was beyond imagination.

Strange indeed, it seemed to me, that Mother should view our nation's capital in that way. Hadn't the United States been founded upon faith in God? That was what I had learned in school. In those days we were not aware that something was going terribly wrong, that this foundation was being deliberately undermined by a new breed of well-meaning educators who sincerely but mistakenly thought that the future could better be built upon humanistic ideals.

In my childhood, faith in God was an accepted part of public education. No one would have considered it a violation of the First Amendment to talk about God in school—least of all Miss Floy Offin! She taught us that faith in our Creator was the foundation of our country. Certainly it was an inseparable part of American history, as we learned it, and intimately woven into the entire fabric of our nation's unique foundation and heritage. Before leaving England in 1606, the first settlers had, in the First Charter of Virginia, referred to their venture as: ". . . so noble a Work. . . by the Providence of Almighty God. . . ." In 1620, the Mayflower Compact declared: "Haveing undertaken for the glorie of God, and advancements of the Christian faith. . . a voyage to plant the first colonie. . . ." Though not an evangelical Christian, Benjamin Franklin had exhorted the drafters of the Constitution: "God governs in the affairs of men. . . without His concurring aid. . . our projects will be confounded. . . I, therefore. . . move that, henceforth, prayers. . . be held in this assembly every morning we proceed to business. . . ." In 1776 the Declaration of Independence appealed in its opening paragraphs to the "self-evident" truth that ". . . all men are created equal, that they are endowed by their Creator with certain inalienable Rights. . . ."

John F. Kennedy's recognition of the existence and authority of God in his inaugural address was only an echo of similar statements made by nearly every one of his predecessors in that great office. In this country's first inaugural addresss, on April 30, 1789, President George Washington declared earnestly: "It would be peculiarly improper to omit in this first official act my fervent supplications to that Almighty Being who rules over the universe. . . ." In his first Thanksgiving proclamation later that year, Washington said: "Whereas it is the duty of all nations to acknowledge the providence of Almighty God, to obey His will, to be grateful for His benefits, and humbly implore His protection and favor. . . ."

Down through the history of this country, political leaders in official capacity have affirmed again and again that these United States of America are founded upon faith in God. It would be dishonest to teach the history of this country in public schools without acknowledging the key role that faith in God has played. To banish God from public schools in the name of the "separation of church and state" would be to destroy the very foundation upon which America was built and would clearly represent a strange new interpretation of the "separation" doctrine never intended by its framers. In his famous Gettysburg Address, President Abraham Lincoln declared that this nation was "conceived in Liberty, and dedicated to the proposition that all men are *created* equal." It is an undeniable fact of history that from the very beginning and consistently thereafter these United States of America were intended to be a "nation *under God*," subject to His will and trusting to His guidance. As Justice William O. Douglas would later affirm, ". . . our institutions presuppose a Supreme Being."*

My childhood was rich with this heritage. The mechanistic theories that human beings are merely biological robots making conditioned responses had not yet taken over in education and government. Respect for individual rights and cooperation among the ranchers in our area was based upon their mutual acceptance of man's

---

* Zorach a Clausen 343 U.S. 306, 313, (1952)

ultimate accountability to his Creator. We would have considered it a gross contradiction to say, "There are no moral absolutes," and in the next breath to complain about what was "wrong" with society. Only in obedience to the laws of God written in our hearts would we find true freedom from slavery to our baser lusts and to oppressive governments.

In that rural schoolhouse we were taught "liberty under law": that to deny God-given moral absolutes would inevitably destroy the liberties we cherished in America. Without law there would be anarchy. But human law that denied accountability to God could only bring tyranny, the imposition of the will of a few upon the many. Moreover, life itself would be meaningless without an identifiable purpose to our existence and the freedom of choice to accept that Creator-given destiny. This was the message of the Declaration of Independence: "... *created* equal and endowed *by their Creator*...." The belief that human beings were not the product of chance, but designed by a God of love, had ignited an unquenchable flame of liberty in the human spirit. God had built into man a freedom that placed his soul beyond the control of totalitarian governments. The human spirit might be broken by force, but it could only be won by love.

This simple belief, which the Founding Fathers had declared to be "self-evident," was a common theme of Bible reading and prayer in our daily family worship. Father quoted 2 Corinthians 3:17 often: "Where the Spirit of the Lord is, there is liberty." He frequently reminded us, "Unless God made us in His image, liberty is a meaningless word!" This simple faith was consistently declared in the patriotic songs we sang at school. I look back now and remember how, with bursting lungs and

deep feeling, we made the rafters shake as we sang lustily
and without shame:

> Our fathers' God, to Thee,
>   Author of liberty,
> To Thee we sing:
>   Long may our land be bright
> With freedom's holy light;
>   Protect us by Thy might,
> Great God, our King!

When I was growing up on the Reed Ranch in
Nebraska, this rich heritage of faith was considered to
be a normal part of life in America. Even then, however,
these foundational values were being eroded in ways we
didn't understand. The growing crime rate in society and
the corruption among police officers and politicians
sworn to uphold the law were still looked upon as an
affront to Almighty God. Unfortunately, however, He was
becoming more often referred to as "our *fathers'* God,"
and less often acknowledged as our own. "Liberty *from*
God" was slowly but surely replacing "liberty *under*
God." Who can now deny the bitter fruit of this new
"emancipation"?

Molded by the simple faith of my parents and the
unflinching commitment of Miss Floy Offin, I was not
yet aware that already in those days faith in God was
becoming less important in daily American life and more
a matter of past tradition. It was still inscribed on our
public buildings and monuments (on the very top of the
Washington Monument, 555 feet high, the words "Praise
be to God!" are still engraved in steel), as well as on
our money. Unfortunately, however, God's name was
inscribed on fewer and fewer hearts. America was
becoming increasingly proud of her power and wealth,

crediting national success more to her own efforts and genius and less to God. As we forgot the basis for past blessings, we became heedless of the warnings from past leaders, such as the one engraved on the Thomas Jefferson Memorial in Washington, D.C.:

> God who gave us life gave us liberty. Can the liberties of a nation be secure when we have removed a conviction that these liberties are the gift of God?

Though few of us in that bygone rural era realized it, the human self was even then being called by such grandiose titles as the "Higher Self" and was gradually taking the place of God. In our State of Nebraska, however, we were confident that the faith upon which America was founded was solidly secure. The Constitution of Nebraska began with these words: "We, the people, grateful to Almighty God for our freedom...." Though some of the traveling Methodist ministers may have hinted at the unthinkable possibility from that schoolhouse pulpit, I don't recall that anyone in my community even suspected that Almighty God might eventually be banished from the very institutions that owed their existence to their founders' faith in Him! However, this was exactly what some farsighted religious leaders apparently began to fear. And to prevent it, they mounted an ill-fated national campaign to establish Christianity by law.

While I was still in grammar school, there was a growing movement throughout the country, supported heavily by William Jennings Bryan, to forbid the teaching of evolution in public schools. A number of states adopted laws forbidding any teacher in a state-supported school or university "to teach any theory that denies the story of the Divine Creation of man as taught in the Bible and to teach instead that man has descended from a lower order of animals." This well-intentioned but misguided attempt to force our forefathers' faith upon their unwilling descendants was unfortunately a denial of the very freedom of choice that the God they believed in had bequeathed to us all. It was doomed to produce exactly the opposite effect that they had intended.

Perhaps if they had been willing to allow evolution to be taught in public schools as a theory and to be frankly discussed in the open, it wouldn't have subsequently gained its almost universal acceptance as "science." An honest examination of the theory would have exposed its fatal flaws and logical consequences: that if our brains, and thus the ideas in our brains, have evolved by chance, then the theory of evolution, being itself the product of random motions of atoms in our brains, had no relationship to truth. Its credibility would of necessity be suspect. At best it could only be argued that the theory of evolution had gained increasing acceptance because it helped the race to survive, though this could hardly be demonstrated scientifically. It could never be demonstrated, however, that the theory was *true*, for truth has no significance in "natural selection" or "survival of the fittest." The only measuring stick is the "survival" of the species, without any ethical basis to declare *why* this survival is of any value.

Nor could *any* theory of science, sociology, psychology, or politics be related to truth, since all ideas could only have evolved by chance in our brains. If evolution were a fact, all schools and especially the very universities where this theory is so highly honored would have to be closed. Education would be at best a misguided attempt to use our brains for the purpose of reasoning, which would be an impossible and meaningless process if our brains were merely lumps of evolved protein molecules programmed to make conditioned responses. If man has no spirit, if mind is the same as brain, if we are not made in the image of God, then love, the appreciation of beautiful music or art, the concepts of truth and justice, are mere chemical reactions of no more significance than a stomach pain or an itch. But if we do have the power of choice, then it is no more right to exclude evolution from theoretical consideration than to exclude creationism.

Few suspected the sudden turn of events that almost overnight discredited in the minds of millions the belief that man was made in the image of God and instead popularized the theory that our race had descended from apelike creatures of uncertain identity. The overzealous attempts by some Christians to restrict freedom in education backfired and gained for the evolutionists a new respectability for their theory. This was a major catalyst in starting the process of eliminating God from education, daily life, and public affairs in the United States.

Twice a Democratic presidential candidate, William Jennings Bryan was greatly admired and respected in our state as a longtime resident of Lincoln, Nebraska. By 1925, however, his former national prestige as a political leader in the Democratic Party was all but gone. Nevertheless, he was still renowned as one of America's greatest orators. No one could have guessed that Bryan's debating skills would fail him as they did in the famous Scopes Trial. Instead of putting evolution to rest once and for all, as he had intended, this trial of the century discredited the faith that Bryan represented and laid the foundation for the final banishment of God from the public school scene.

Had it not been for the submitting in court of certain

"evidence," later discredited, Bryan might have survived the withering cross-examination of Clarence Darrow. However, Bryan had been left speechless, completely devastated, when a certain tooth had been "definitely identified" as belonging to the so-called "Nebraska Man." Zealous imaginations "reconstructed" this single tooth into an entire species and gave it the impressive name *Hesperopithecus haroldcookii*. The existence of this important "missing link," "scientifically established" by expert testimony in court, validated evolution and discredited the idea of special creation that Jennings had argued should be the only "origin of man" taught in public schools.

Though excluded from the jury, the statements of scientists supporting evolution were made part of the court record and received wide publicity, as did Darrow's clever ridicule of Bryan's belief in the literal account of creation in Genesis. That the judge found Scopes guilty of violating the law against teaching evolution and fined him 100 dollars was small comfort to Bryan, who knew he had lost the real case. Darrow had succeeded in placing the Bible on trial before the entire United States and had won an overwhelming victory-by-ridicule for agnosticism.

My parents, as well as most of the other ranchers, followed the trial with great interest, although I don't believe they understood its far-reaching significance at that time. It was Bryan's most humiliating and bitter personal defeat, one from which he never recovered. Five days after the court's decision, he died in his sleep, without ever learning that "Nebraska Man" was later proven to be a pig! It was decades after Bryan's death before the true identification of this important tooth became widely known. But by then evolution had gained too firm a foothold in public schools, universities, and minds to be discredited by any evidence, no matter how overwhelming. Though Neanderthal Man would later be acknowledged to be fully human and not a "missing link" after all, and though Piltdown Man, Java Man, and Peking Man would all eventually be exposed as frauds, they would remain forever enshrined in minds, museums, and textbooks as "proof" of evolution.

Those who believe that human beings are highly-evolved, complex conglomerations of DNA and protein programmed by experience to make conditioned responses have done an exceptional job of conditioning the general public to accept their fanciful theories. Opinions can be manufactured and manipulated, but history cannot be altered. It is a historical fact that this nation owes its existence and the unique freedom that made it great to its Founding Fathers' faith in God. As that faith molded this country in the past, so will present beliefs decide America's future. The controversy between evolution and creation is far more than academic. Evolution destroys the only basis for law itself. Of course I didn't understand this at the time, any more than I could have known that the legal profession would become my career. Carrying a warning as well as a promise, the Declaration of Independence defines the basis of human rights and ultimate law very clearly:

> We hold these truths to be self-evident, that all men are *created* equal; that they are endowed *by their Creator* with certain unalienable rights; that among these are life, liberty, and the pursuit of happiness. . . .
>
> We, therefore, the Representatives of the United States of America, in general Congress assembled, appealing to the *Supreme Judge* of the world for the rectitude of our intentions,

do . . . [place] firm reliance on the protection of
Divine Providence . . . [emphasis added].

Our faith in God brought our family through a major
crisis when my father suffered a stroke. I was ten years
old and remember only too well Dr. Priemer's sudden
arrival, his solemn expression as he hurried into the bedroom where Father lay, and the anxiety and bewilder-
ment I felt as we waited and prayed. Although he made
a good recovery, Father never regained the full use of
his right arm and no longer had the strength to continue
the vigorous life and responsibilities demanded by the
ranch. It was a sad day for all of us when those beloved
2000 acres were sold and we moved away.

With brief residences in one small town after another,
the next few years were an unsettling contrast to the
stable life we had known on the ranch. Father had been
a lay Methodist minister. Now that he was free from the
confining demands of crops and herds, he began to
receive calls to pastor congregations, first in Wauneta,
then in Eustis, and later in Oshkosh—all in Nebraska. In
1929 we moved to beautiful Colorado Springs, Colorado,
where father bought a comfortable house with an inspiring view of Pike's Peak, snowcapped most of the year.
What a contrast it was to the broad, level plains of
Nebraska! I had suffered from severe attacks of hay fever
on the ranch, but here in the clear mountain air my health
and vigor improved dramatically.

It was in Colorado Springs that Father joined the
Church of the Nazarene. I was especially unhappy about
the change, but Dad's decisions were not open to appeal.
We Reed boys didn't fully understand the theological
differences that forced him as a matter of conscience to
make the change. More important for me was having to
leave old friends and begin the slow and sometimes

painful process of making new ones. The confusion which this brought added to my growing teenage resentment of parental restrictions and control.

When we moved to Colorado Springs, my parents had enrolled me in a religious academy. It went only to the eighth grade, for which I was grateful. Upon entering public high school, the greater freedom and its accompanying temptations were a contrast that I began to enjoy. I had chafed at the many moves from town to town and church to church since leaving the ranch, and had begun to let my rebellion be known by demanding greater freedom at home. When I was midway through high school, Father was assigned to pastor the Nazarene Church at Fowler, Colorado, a picturesque little town of 2000 on the Arkansas River, east of Pueblo. This latest move only increased my confusion and rebellion.

Life on the ranch had involved long hours and hard work that at times had seemed monotonous drudgery. By contrast, life in the city seemed empty at times and lacking in purpose, and that only added to the uncertainties that plagued me as a teenager growing into adulthood. I "fell in love" for the first time, and suddenly life was filled with the heady joys of romance. Generously allowed the use of the family Model A Ford, I began to stay out later than the time my parents had set. There were warnings and a continuing battle of wits as I tried to stretch my freedom to new limits. One day, in a wild, impulsive, show-off spree, I raced the car around in a dusty field and brought it home filthy—and late. Father decided it was time to teach me a hard lesson.

The high school Junior-Senior Banquet was the biggest social event of the year. My girlfriend, Elizabeth, and I had looked forward to it for weeks. Of course I had been promised the car for that evening. However, on the long-awaited day of the banquet Father made an announcement that shattered my dreams.

"You understand that you're not taking the car to-night," he informed me in a tone that I knew didn't allow for negotiation.

"But you promised . . . weeks ago . . . the Banquet . . . I've been counting on it!" I protested in mock shock. I had secretly suspected this might happen but had been afraid to bring up the subject for fear that it might tip the scale in the wrong direction. It had seemed better to keep quiet. I now wholeheartedly regretted that strategy.

"That promise had conditions. You nearly wrecked the car the last time!" Father reminded me.

"I was sorry about that . . . and still am." I fumbled for words. "What about Elizabeth? I told her I'd have the car. . . ." My protest sputtered to a halt. Trying to persuade him might be taken as a further sign of rebellion and bring worse consequences.

"You seem to have forgotten the importance of relia-bility and responsibility, George," he added slowly. There was a sadness in his voice. "You have to learn that there are consequences to what you do, and you have to face them." I knew he was doing what was right even though he shared my painful disappointment.

It was too late to make arrangements to ride with someone else. There was nothing to do but walk Elizabeth to and from the school. That was humiliating enough for the biggest event of the year, but to make matters even worse, coming home we were caught in a driving rain that ruined her party dress and made me a special object of her mother's wrath. It was a hard lesson. Perhaps that's why I never forgot it.

I had always been content to imagine that being a member of the Reed family and being a Christian were somewhat synonymous. The growing conflict between what I wanted to be and do and the unflinching standards which my parents set made me realize at last that one's relationship with God is a personal matter and doesn't run in the family. My parents didn't try to force their beliefs upon me. It was a matter of example and education. They lived by their convictions, and so long as we boys were part of the family living at home, we were expected to respect those standards. They were wise enough to try to guide us without driving us.

Sometimes after I had failed to live up to what my parents expected, I later learned that they knew of my misconduct all along. They kept quiet because they knew that my conscience would deal with me better than they could. Many a time, when tempted to violate the "Reed code of ethics," I was prevented by remembering the times I had overheard my parents tell friends and relatives, "Our four sons are such a joy to us . . . they're so dependable!"

It was during a revival at the Nazarene Church in Colorado Springs that I finally made the most important decision of my life. The evangelist didn't say anything new, but there was a spiritual power, a clarity of expression, and a deep conviction in what he said that drove God's truth at last into the deepest recesses of my heart. It became crystal clear that there were only two possible explanations for my existence: I was either a cosmic accident, or God had created me for a purpose.

I knew that the first possibility did not explain the universe either within the atom or the far-flung galaxies, much less the intricate complexity of a single cell. If everything resulted from blind chance, that would reduce to absurdity love, justice, and all else that gave life meaning. In my conscience I knew that I had violated the moral laws of my Creator and that I could never fulfill the purpose of the priceless existence He had entrusted to me except in loving submission to His will.

My inner rebellion against God's laws and my desire to be a god unto myself became so obvious that I felt an overwhelming sense of shame, as though all my secret thoughts were exposed before God and there was no place for me to hide. I knew that living a perfect life in the future, even if that were possible, would never make up for past violations of conscience. I had offended Infinite Justice and therefore owed an infinite debt, which I as a finite being could never pay. For the first time I realized why God had become a man—so that He, the unique God-man, could die in my place and pay a debt that I could not. I heard Christ knocking at the door of my heart, offering to forgive me and to come into my spirit to live His resurrected life in and through me. I invited Him in, received Him as my Savior, and asked Him to be my Lord, pledging to follow wherever He would lead me.

Father's illness had brought us back to Colorado Springs after it had become impossible for him to fulfill his duties as pastor of the church in Fowler. Shortly after we moved back into the same home with the breathtaking view of Pike's Peak, he underwent surgery. The doctors found inoperable cancer and sent him home to die. Those were sad yet triumphant days as Father proved the reality of his faith by the way he faced death. He reminded us that he was going away to be with Christ in a new dimension of life in heaven, beyond the pain and sorrow and disappointments of earth. He would wait there for the day when the rest of us would join him. On September 15, 1933, at the age of 72, Father said farewell to us and went to be with the Savior he had loved and served so faithfully.

5

Romance and Reality

A man's heart deviseth his way: but the Lord directeth his steps.

How often the hopeful dreams of youthful idealism bloom only briefly, then wither and fade away. Entering adulthood is never easy. It was especially traumatic for those who made this difficult transition during the bleak depression years of the 1930's. The scarcity of jobs frustrated determined, honest effort and bred a hopeless resignation that choked talent and ambition. How many thousands during those deadening years lost and never regained the hope and confidence they needed for making their lives count.

Fortunately, I escaped being part of those tragic statistics. The years of spartan training on the ranch under Father's watchful eye were now a priceless asset. His insistence that there was no excuse for "giving up," and the inspiration of his undying trust in God no matter how hopeless or impossible the odds, spared me the inertia that had settled upon much of middle America. Being able to do "all things through Christ who strengthens me" was an outlook and a conviction I had seen demonstrated in the lives of my parents. In my own tentative steps toward maturity, there came times when I experienced the periods of uncertainty that plague even those most eager to do His will. Those were battles I fought on my knees in prayer. I learned that faith to face any trial was not a mental attitude I created in order to claim a blessing, but trust and guidance that grew out of a love relationship with my Lord.

Ever since being uprooted from our ranch, we four Reed brothers had felt a strange restlessness. It had stirred us anew each time we had moved to another town and home. Perhaps it had been this sense of rootlessness as much as a desire for adventure that had taken my two older brothers all the way out to Southern California. Harold had returned to Colorado, but not Edwin. He had fallen in love with a California girl. This new relationship had not only changed his life but would affect mine as well. Wedding plans were made, and I was included in them.

Little did I suspect the many consequences that were involved for my own life. Such are the ways of God, who often nudges us to take a major step when we are least aware that He is leading us down a precise path of His choosing. Looking back on many such turning points in my life, I came into a practical understanding of those favorite verses of Father's from Proverbs 3 that he had drilled into us as children:

> Trust in the Lord with all thine heart, and lean not unto thine own understanding. In all thy ways acknowledge Him, and He shall direct thy paths.

Nothing had been farther from my mind than visiting California. It seemed like another planet, light years from Colorado. The glamorous, the bizarre, the slightly unreal —they were all there to be savored in that fabled place. Where else could you surf in the morning, ski in the afternoon, and pick oranges in the fabulous sunset? When my brother requested my presence as best man at his wedding, my response was an immediate and joyous "Yes." I felt as if I were on the verge of some unnameable and intriguing venture when at last I climbed into the car along with Wesley and Mom on that July morning of 1934.

Given the primitive state both of the roads and of automobile engineering in those days, such a trip was a major undertaking. In our state-of-the-art 1930 Model A Ford we managed with no small difficulty to navigate the steep and winding route across the rugged Rocky Mountains and down onto the high desert of Utah and Arizona.

We weren't alone on that tortuous route. During those years a regular procession of decrepit and desperately-pieced-together vehicles was fleeing the boarded-up farms and closed factories of America's heartland. The call to "Go West, young man" was heeded by the aged and the aging as well, and with them went the children, the young mothers soon to give birth, the empty-eyed losers, the gamblers, the incurably optimistic. That narrow strip of asphalt revealed an ever-unfolding drama of life at its most desperate—and most hopeful.

It was a long and exhausting week. At times the road we traversed was like a heated griddle that fried our tires one by one, and our boiling radiator demanded frequent halts on the steep grades. After one final tire change in the broiling sun of the Mojave Desert just inside the California border, we struggled at last with a wheezing engine up over the old Cajon Pass, and with great relief began our descent into San Bernardino.

Spread before our wondering eyes was a strange new world known to us only from travel folders. Stretching to the horizon, the lush valley was a green and golden checkerboard of orange, lemon, and grapefruit groves bordered with eucalyptus, palm, and other exotic trees. The thousands of acres of citrus were clustered in special areas, and in between grew every imaginable variety of other fruit trees, vegetables, and brilliantly blooming flowers. Nothing more was needed to convince us weary travelers that, exactly as we had heard rumored, California did indeed flow with milk, honey, and orange juice.

We had not driven far in this almost-unbelievable paradise when Wesley spotted a sign that read: "All the orange juice you can drink for ten cents." I pulled the old Model A over to the side of the road in front of the stand. Pointing to the sign, Wesley called to the proprietor, "Hey, do you mean, uh . . . *all* you can drink?"

Assured that we hadn't misread the invitation, we laid out our three dimes and proceeded to gulp down one glass after another of the best orange juice we had ever tasted. When a week's thirst had at last been quenched, we drove on our way, leaving the entrepreneur contemplating the wisdom of raising his price or changing the terms.

On July 26, 1934, my brother Edwin was married to Lillian Hoyt in a beautiful ceremony at the First Methodist Church of Pasadena. The wedding over, we succumbed to the temptation to linger. Better give the old Model A a rest—and we weren't in any hurry to head back across the deserts and mountains. Besides, Wesley and I were growing rather fond of California, and there were no jobs or even prospects of any compelling us to return. Mother happily agreed.

Without even trying, I landed a job. Against all odds,

Edwin had managed to find higher-paying work that was more in keeping with his new responsibilities as a married man, and I inherited his former prestigious position as chauffeur to Miss Minford, a wealthy Pasadena socialite. To a country boy like me, raised on a farm in Nebraska, it was heady stuff to work for a member of high society, one who lived in what seemed to me a veritable mansion.

I had the honor of chauffeuring this distinguished lady about the greater Los Angeles area. Unfortunately, the maps I pored over didn't seem to bear any relationship to the maze of street signs that flew past the limousine window and only added to the confusion and frustration that this sprawling megalopolis created in the mind of a small-town boy trying to bluff his way around the big city. Our disastrous jaunts added up to one too many, and Miss Minford politely informed me she had found another driver.

We had already stayed in California far longer than any of us had originally planned. At the time I didn't understand the "something" that seemed to detain us. Only later would I begin to comprehend that this was part of God's purpose for my life, lovingly and wisely determined long before I ever knew Him.

In spite of the heavy unemployment, Wesley refused to give up; he would show me how to land a job. And he did—delivering hundred-pound chunks of ice for the Pasadena Ice Company. Since Wesley had proven to be such a hard worker, the boss figured he couldn't go wrong hiring his brother. Though smaller, I was no less eager, and we tried to outdo each other on the job. Our dripping burdens weren't welcome in elevators, and it was often a race up several flights of stairs to see who could make it first. Soaked with sweat and melting ice, we lugged our loads side by side. By the end of the summer we were in absolutely top physical condition.

Although it had been my plan to return in time to register at the University of Colorado in Boulder, where I had anticipated having an athletic scholarship, Labor Day 1934 found us still lingering on in California. Now, instead of standing in line to register for classes in far-off Colorado, I found myself at a picnic in Tournament Park with Pasadena's First Church of the Nazarene. It was hot, even in the shade, where I was cooling off with a Coke after a game of softball.

"I'm Orton Wiley." I became aware of a smiling little man approaching me, hand extended. "You're George Reed. I've heard a lot about you." Then, as he saw the questioning look on my face, he added, "All of it good, I can assure you. That's why I want to talk to you."

Although we had never met, I immediately recognized him as the highly revered Nazarene theologian and President of Pasadena College. It was a complete surprise to me that he even knew of my existence.

"Roy Stevens is very impressed with your athletic ability and experience," Dr. Wiley continued. "On his recommendation, I'd like to offer you a job as his assistant for the coming year."

I was flabbergasted. It didn't make sense. I had a slight acquaintance with Roy Stevens, the Athletic Director of Pasadena College, who had apparently talked to Dr. Wiley about me. "That's a great honor," I stammered in reply, "but. . .well, I've really been planning to attend the University of Colorado. . . . In fact, I should be leaving any day now to go back there to register. . . ." What was I saying? I should have been there already if I really intended what I'd said.

Dr. Wiley patted me on the shoulder and with a knowing wink and a smile suggested, "Think it over— and pray about it. Then come in to see me next week. I'll be praying too."

Mother had already been doing a lot of praying that seemed to be producing fast and astonishing results. She, of course, couldn't possibly have known exactly what God had in mind—for example, that Wesley was destined to become a Los Angeles Superior Court Judge—nor how it would come about. What she did seem to know, however, and with unshakable conviction, was that He had brought us all out to California for His own definite purpose. I had overheard her praying on her knees in her bedroom that her two younger boys would enter Pasadena College, a Nazarene institution. Was this job offer an answer to that prayer?

Wesley and I prayed together and talked it over. With the assurance that this was God's will, and the promise of financial backing from Mother, we both enrolled as freshmen at Pasadena College (now Pt. Loma Nazarene College). A beautiful confirmation of this step was that the salary I earned as assistant to the Director of Athletics turned out to be considerably more than I would have received from my athletic scholarship at the University of Colorado. I was still learning—slowly and at times painfully, but ever more willingly—that God's way was best.

Mother sold the house in Colorado Springs and bought a home in Pasadena. Out of her savings she loaned Wesley and me the money to purchase a small oil business, which we ran as partners. This was a bold venture for depression days, but by God's grace and with much prayer and perseverance it turned out to be the right decision. Wesley attended his classes in the mornings and delivered heating oil, kerosene, distillate, and paint thinner to our customers in the afternoon. Three days a week I attended classes and taught gymnastics. The other two days and Saturdays I joined Wesley in the business, and eventually we saw our efforts begin to turn a small profit.

Promoted to the position of Athletic Director in my junior year, I enlarged the department to provide a full physical education program for every student. Although intercollegiate athletics hadn't yet been approved by the Board of Trustees, with the backing of President Wiley we entered small-college competition in basketball, and with my six-foot-four brother Wesley at center, we won about half our games that first year. Pasadena College has since built a solid reputation as a basketball power. Four years later, in 1940, I was elected president of the Pasadena College Alumni Association and won approval for a full program of intercollegiate athletics.

Some amazing changes had taken place since we had begun that fateful journey out West to Edwin's wedding. School, jobs, acquaintances—there had been a complete turnaround in my life. There would be another, and that involved the decision to change my major to Sociology and Criminology.

My chief inspiration for this new direction was Dr. Adele Steele, former Commissioner of Corrections for the Philippines and a Columbia University professor. This awesomely accredited but humble and warmhearted lady took a personal interest in me. Under her instruction, the field of penology and corrections opened up the exciting possibility of doing something really significant with my life. Dr. Steele was far from an ivory-tower idealist. Her concepts were based on reality, and she trained her students to recognize the workable and discard the impractical. During those exciting last two years of college she led us on visits to all of the major penal institutions and correctional facilities in the State of California. By the time I graduated, in 1938, I had been introduced through this dedicated reformer to all the leaders in my chosen field throughout the Golden State.

There was a second event that made my junior year a

red letter one and which changed the entire course of my life. In the fall semester a coed from Ashland, Oregon, had transferred from Idaho's Northwest Nazarene College to Pasadena College. It was a few months before Lois Goetz and I became acquainted and a few more before we had our first date. When summer rolled around, I noted with elation that Lois decided to stay on with friends rather than return to her home in Oregon. I knew her well enough by then to understand that she too had placed herself completely in her loving Father's hands and was trusting Him to guide her life.

It was a dizzy schedule that commenced with my senior year. Being Director of Athletics, carrying a full 16 hours of college credits, helping to keep the Reed brothers' oil company afloat, and courting the sweetest girl in all the State of California—it was more than a challenge. I would have preferred to make the latter a full-time occupation, but I had to remind myself that the Reed clan were a practical bunch. We'd been brought up that way.

Lois and I left the campus musical in a dreamy mood that rainy night of December 10, 1937. The production, "The Night Shall Be Filled With Music," was neither great dramatically nor great musically, but it suited our mood. Humming snatches of melody, recollecting bits of dialogue, we searched for a cafe.

Ending a date with something to eat was the expected order of events, I knew, but I had something so much more important on my mind. When we were at last seated in a late-night eatery, I could scarcely interpret the menu. By the time we'd sloshed back to the car and driven a few soggy miles into the foothills above Pasadena, the question could no longer be delayed. "Lois, darling, would you take your chances with me for life?" Tears and raindrops glistened together as she quietly nodded her head. Some minutes later I awoke to the fact that I was engaged—and ecstatically happy. Success in my tough senior year now had an added significance for me, and when in May of 1938 we both received our diplomas, the reality of sharing life's major steps together seemed all the sweeter.

That same month I sat with 800 other young men and women in a large examination room, staring down at the three-hour Civil Service exam before me. My competitors and I were all vying for the three positions being offered by the Los Angeles Probation Department. At that moment I wondered whether I really wanted that job as a deputy probation officer. Was it worth the effort to take the exam when the odds were so slim? "I can do *all* things through Christ," the Holy Spirit prompted me, and I began to write.

Two weeks later, almost afraid to see what it said, I ripped open a letter from the Los Angeles County Civil Service Commission and let out a whoop of joy. I had tied for second place! My job assignment was to be a counselor at Juvenile Forestry Camp Number Five in the foothills above La Verne on the western edge of Los Angeles.

Best of all, it meant that Lois and I could now set our wedding date. On October 10, 1938, a beautifully clear fall night, we said our vows before my oldest brother, Dr. Harold Reed, in the Wee Kirk of the Heather in Glendale. Later, when we sat holding hands in the moonlight in the Kirk's traditional "Wishing Chair," our hearts were full of gratitude to the One who had brought us together—Lois from Oregon and me from Colorado—to meet the way He had planned. There was no way we could even imagine what lay down the road, but we shared the same strong conviction that God was taking us somewhere special.

We spent our first Thanksgiving apart. A forest fire was raging above Pacific Palisades and I was there battling it with 30 of my boys. The outdoor environment, the physical energy demanded, and the element of shared risk made this type of assignment a healthy outlet for these young men who so desperately needed redirection for their lives. The record bore that out. The rehabilitative success record for these Forestry Camp grads was 80 percent during the five years it had been in operation. Somehow my life became intertwined with theirs. I felt I was saying goodbye to "family" when I was promoted to Regional Supervisor for the Los Angeles County Juvenile Court program for the entire East Los Angeles-San Gabriel Valley area.

Though the scope of my responsibility had broadened tremendously, I was still able to deal very personally with the juveniles under my jurisdiction. It was rewarding beyond measure to see a young man off probation for a year or two walk into my office with a young wife and perhaps a first baby to share with me his joy and satisfaction at having become a worthwhile citizen. My own joy was no less.

6

Treachery in the Pacific

Then they cry unto the Lord in their trouble,
and He bringeth them out of their distresses. . . .
Oh that men would praise the Lord for his
goodness, and for His wonderful works to the
children of men!

The insistent jangle of the hall phone took my attention
from the reassuring sounds coming from the kitchen. We
had just come in from church, and Lois was fixing dinner
that peaceful Sunday in December of 1941. The words
I heard from the other end of the line would remain forever etched on my memory: "The Japanese are attacking
Pearl Harbor!"

As the events of that "day of infamy," as Roosevelt was
to call it, unfolded, my fellow Americans and I sat glued
to our radios in utter disbelief. In all, 19 warships had
been hit and the lives of over 2000 naval officers and their
men had been lost. In less than two hours the whole strategic defense system in the Pacific had been virtually

wiped out. And all this while Japanese diplomats were in Washington D.C. pretending to be discussing in good faith with representatives of the United States government the settlement of differences between the two countries.

Congress lost no time in declaring war on Japan, and the nation joined heart and muscle to mount its defenses. Black days followed. Island after island in the strategic South Pacific was overrun under savage suicide attacks that overwhelmed brave but outnumbered and outgunned defenders. Guam and Wake went quickly. Mighty Corregidor fell, and Malaysia, Hong Kong, Burma, Singapore, Sumatra, and Java as well. There were other casualties to the Japanese juggernaut, hitherto unknown to the average American. Their exotic names became household words—Rabaul, Bougainville, Iwo Jima, Enewitok.

It was hard to stay at home, no matter how important the task, when other men were laying down their lives in the steaming jungles and watery expanses of the Pacific arena. If democracy was worth living for, it had to be worth dying for. In October of the next year I stood beside my brother, John Wesley, in the Federal Building in Los Angeles as together we were sworn in as chief petty officers in the U.S. Navy and took the oath to defend our country against all enemies. Afterward, between hugs and congratulations from our families, we exuberantly related to a roving radio interviewer just how we were going to win the war.

After goodbyes to wives and family, Wesley and I left for Norfolk, Virginia, to train as athletic specialists under Commander Gene Tunney of boxing fame. It was tough. From office desks to push-ups and ten-mile runs was a painful transition, but eight weeks later we graduated, once again in top physical condition, and left for our assignments.

At the new Naval Training Station in Bainbridge, Maryland, I was immediately able to put my own training to work. I was assigned Company Commander over 120 raw recruits, and at the end of eight intensive weeks my first company graduated and was inspected by the Admiral of the First Naval District. I was able to train four more companies before being reassigned.

The ivy halls of Cornell were a far cry from the raw newness of Bainbridge. Lois and I look back on those days with a special nostalgia. Initially transferred in June of 1943 to serve as athletic director, I was later appointed educational officer at the Naval Officers' Training command at Cornell University in Ithaca, New York. My job was to serve as liaison between university and Navy in order to train bright young men to become qualified naval officers in the shortest time possible. I was happy with my job. My commanding officer, Captain John Chippendale, wasn't. In his own words, he had been " . . . put in dry dock on the hills of Cornell high above the waters of Lake Cayuga.''

A major part of the satisfaction I felt with my work at Cornell was having Lois with me. We had a small apartment in the home of motherly Mrs. Mattocks, whose greatest delight was in treating us as her own children. The old-world campus itself, its excellent facilities, the beauty of the countryside, and the friendships formed there seemed almost a contradiction in terms when one considers that elsewhere during those same 18 months fellow-Americans were dying on Italian beachheads, and inch by bloody inch were wresting back what Hitler and Hirohito had claimed for their own. I too was in "drydock,'' but I gave everything I had to prepare my men to help finish the job out there as quickly as possible. My final tour of duty was at Sampson Naval Training Center in New York. There I trained a further 5000 recruits to become fit and able fighting men.

On April 12, 1945, Lois and I were just leaving for a birthday dinner date when the radio announced the death, at Warm Springs, Georgia, of our great wartime leader, President Roosevelt. It was a staggering blow. Death never comes at a convenient time. It seemed that this one came at an impossible time. The Allied drive across Europe, which had begun on the Normandy beaches, was a year old and was on the verge of culminating in the battle for Berlin.

Roosevelt's death, in fact, generated an ecstasy of hope (albeit brief) among Hitler's henchmen. Was this the turning point that Hitler's astrologers had foretold? Millions of Americans, on the other hand, were given cause to remember the ringing affirmation of their dead President's first inaugural address more than ten years before: "The only thing we have to fear is fear itself." They determined to redouble their efforts on the home front and on the battlefield.

The end came more suddenly than any of us had dreamed. It had been a long, bloody three months since Germany's capitulation on VE Day, May 7, 1945. The death of the President hadn't slowed our military momentum, but the war in the Pacific promised to be lengthy, with a costly toll of human life on both sides. Because of this, our new president, Harry S. Truman, decided to end the war by unleashing the atomic bomb. It was a momentous decision for a man who hadn't even known of the existence of such a device on the day he had taken office three weeks before.

That historic executive order from the Commander-in-Chief spelled death for 80,000 citizens of Hiroshima and wounded or maimed 240,000 more. Two days later a second bomb was dropped on Nagasaki, killing another 40,000. This terrifying new instrument of destruction changed life forever for all the inhabitants of our planet. Emperor Hirohito spoke prophetically when he declared in his capitulation speech, "To continue the war under these conditions would not only lead to the annihilation of Our Nation, but the destruction of human civilizations as well. . . ."

At the surrender ceremonies in Tokyo Bay, General Douglas MacArthur spoke in the same somber vein:

> Today the guns are silent. A great tragedy has ended. A great victory has been won. The skies no longer rain death—the seas bear only commerce. Men everywhere walk upright in the sunlight. The entire world is quietly at peace.
>
> Men since the beginning of time have sought peace, [but] military alliances, balances of power, Leagues of Nations, all in turn failed, leaving the only path to be by way of the crucible of war. Now we have had our last chance.
>
> If we do not now devise some greater and more equitable system, Armageddon will be at our door.

My heart beat high as I listened. Just as totally as I had given myself to the war effort, I now longed to see a lasting peace established. I had an added stake in my world's future: Lois was pregnant. Along with the thrill of approaching parenthood was the nagging question: What kind of world would this young life inherit? The joyous frenzy as thousands of civilians and sailors danced in the streets at Sampson on VJ night would give way to sober realities, I knew. Wars did not always end when the shooting stopped.

For me, it wasn't the quick return to civilian life I had envisioned. When I put Lois on the train for California to await the birth of our child in January, I didn't realize that the demobilization process would last a weary 3½ months before my discharge papers finally arrived and I boarded the train to join her.

Taking up life where I had left off as Deputy Probation Officer for Los Angeles County wasn't without its hitches. I discovered that a young 4F with very little experience had climbed the department ladder during my three-year absence and was now my superior. The situation wasn't unusual, given the wartime necessity of filling the gaps left by enlistees, and tensions were understandable. I determined, however, that pride would not stand in the way of the goals I had set, and I joined the tens of thousands of young men who were returning to school under the G.I. Bill. For me it meant evening classes at the University of Southern California after a heavy day on the job.

Even these hard times were part of God's foreordained and loving plan for me. It was there, while majoring in Sociology, Criminology, and Pre-Law, that I met Dr. Emory S. Bogardus, Dean of the university's Graduate School.* We became lifelong friends. Years later, when I was Chairman of the United States Parole Board, many of my talks were published and I always sent Dr. Bogardus a copy. Weeks later I would receive the printed talk back, with appropriate comments—some complimentary and some critical. Always, however, there was a short note of encouragement to his former student and friend. Yes, Bogardus was still grading my papers long years after I had left his classroom!

Thoughts of career and hopes of advancement took a back seat when Lois awakened me at four o'clock on the

---

* In 1956, I was granted an L.L.D. degree by Pasadena College and in 1958 an L.L.D. degree by Eastern Nazarene College. On March 1, 1965, I was elected a "Fellow" by the American Society of Criminology for research in a study on the causes of juvenile and youth offenders crime.

morning of January 31, 1946. Her labor pains had started. In celebration of this momentous occasion, she stuck a rose in her hastily combed hair while I brought the car around. I wasted little time warming the engine. My excitement will be understood only by those who have also experienced fatherhood. My role was to get Lois to Pasadena Huntington Hospital—fast. I did. Once there, the hours wore on—morning into afternoon, afternoon into evening. I prayed. The nurse's advice to "relax" went unheeded.

"You are the father of a fine, healthy baby boy." It was 9:35 P.M., and a smiling nurse was handing me a very pink, very precious little bundle. When I joined Lois, I expressed our thankfulness to God that He had answered our earnest prayers.

Later that night as I drove home, my car seemed a hallowed place as I offered up prayer after prayer for this little life entrusted to Lois's and my care. Those were emotionally charged miles as I began to realize the responsibilities that were now mine. I wanted so earnestly to be a good and godly father to my son. Although I have not always succeeded in my life's goals, I have, with God's help, reserved as my top priority a determination to make good on my prayers that night. God did honor those pleas, and that infant son I held so proudly on the night of his birth has turned into a fine, dedicated young Christian man who today is the pride and joy of his parents. His lovely wife, Jane, and their own fine sons, Jesse and Joel, have completed our family circle. God is indeed good.

Events moved rapidly that spring. During the war, Governor Earl Warren had appointed Chief Los Angeles County Probation Officer Karl Holton as head of the newly authorized California Youth Authority, our country's first statewide coordinated delinquency prevention, diagnosis, and treatment program. He had taken to

Sacramento as his deputy director my very good friend and co-worker Herman Stark, who was placed in charge of the Field Services Division of Probation, Parole, Forestry Camps, and Delinquency Prevention. At his suggestion, I applied and successfully tested for an administrative position as a field representative for the C.Y.A.

Because of my earlier experience, I was placed in charge of a statewide Juvenile Forestry Camp program for delinquents. It proved to be an exciting and challenging job. As a result of ever-increasing court commitments, the juveniles involved grew in number, and the program became recognized by many penologists as the most effective method for treating youths in conflict with the law.

One of the keys to the program was hard work. Many of the young men had never known the satisfaction of sustained honest labor. Nor did we just invent something to keep them busy; what they did was vital to the community and the environment. Firebreaks, dams, and emergency mountain roads were developed, along with muscles and callouses. Individual counseling and athletic and education programs left the men no idle time. As a result, these young men matured rapidly and gained a new respect for authority and constructive labor. Upon release from the camps, they returned home under the supervision and guidance of their probation officers.

My professional philosophy as an administrator in the criminal court system was formed during my years under Holton and Stark. Karl Holton had a deep empathy for the thousands of juvenile and youth offenders under his jurisdiction. At the same time, his staff respected him as a strict, no-nonsense administrator. Herman Stark, on the other hand, brought out the best in us through his unfailing warmth and personal charm. My admiration for these two mentors was such that I early adopted a philosophy of correctional administration that I trust to some degree encompassed a balance of both their strengths.

Life at this point seemed all I could desire—a lovely wife, a baby son, an exciting job working with many of California's leading citizens in a new and dynamic program. I certainly wasn't seeking new worlds to conquer that fall of 1948, but God was preparing me for a radical move that would expand my vision and my ministry beyond anything I had ever dreamed.

7
Fear No Man

The fear of the Lord is the beginning of knowledge; but fools despise wisdom and instruction.

We sat entranced, watching the gloriously brilliant floral confections float by. It was New Year's Day, 1949. Surrounded by family and friends at the Tournament of Roses Parade in Pasadena, I basked in the 70-degree sunshine and reveled in the beauty of it all. The next day Lois and I and little George Calvert, aged two, would be heading by car for freezing Minnesota and a new life.

That transition was linked to the 1948 election of Luther W. Youngdahl as Governor of Minnesota. He had campaigned and won on a platform of improved education and mental health and the reorganization of the state's penal program. The Model Youth Corrections Act, similar to the California Youth Authority, had just been passed by the State Legislature, and they were looking for someone to serve as Deputy Director and Chief of

Prevention and Parole Services for the Minnesota Youth Conservation Commission. With the strong backing of Governor Earl Warren, Karl Holton, and Herman Stark, I headed East for the necessary interviews.

Once there, I faced in rapid succession, it seemed, the whole power structure of the State of Minnesota. When Governor Youngdahl declared that I was the man he wanted for the job, my mind was made up as well. The position of Deputy Director of the Youth Conservation Commission for the State of Minnesota was an exciting assignment that would involve a considerable increase in both salary and responsibility. Above all, it would be an opportunity to establish in a new state the correctional programs that had proven so beneficial to troubled youth in California.

The day we arrived in Saint Paul, the temperature was 20 degrees below zero. Two-year-old George was crying and begging to go home. Lois was holding back the tears. We had left home and sun and loved ones for *this*?

First impressions were quickly dissipated as I came to know and appreciate Luther Youngdahl. Never had a governor taken such an active role in publicizing and promoting his dream of a truly dynamic and effective youth conservation program. Every Saturday night he addressed the citizens of Minnesota on his televised "Governor's Report to the People." He would present a dramatized case history of a youth in conflict with society, and then outline how the new Youth Conservation Commission was dealing with problems such as his. The Governor's approach was to gain popular backing from the people, not through sterile statistics, but with the impelling reality of broken lives restored to new hope.

Youngdahl's support became a tremendous encouragement and incentive in further developing the program. We had jurisdiction over all juvenile and youthful offenders to age 25. We operated the Red Wing Training School for Boys, the Sauk Center School for Girls, the Women's Reformatory at Shakope, and the Saint Cloud Men's Reformatory. It was a good start, but much more was needed! I immediately set to work to reorganize and expand the entire program.

Two weeks after assuming my job, we presented to the legislature a greatly enlarged statewide probation and parole program, Community Delinquency Prevention Services, and two new diagnostic centers. The latter were designed to provide a complete clinical diagnostic study of all new juvenile and youthful offenders before placing them in an individualized training and treatment program. Part of that treatment would involve reforestation work in two new forestry camps in Minnesota's vast northern woodland.

Soon the Governor was sending me to fill many of his speaking engagements, and I thus became acquainted with community leaders throughout the state. The Governor's Youth Conference in Saint Paul in the fall of 1950 drew some 2000 children, youth, and adults for its three days of sessions. With so many members of the State Legislature there, as well as all the figures prominent in Minnesota's juvenile reform movement, and with very favorable press and TV coverage, we were hopeful that the 1950-51 legislative session would pass our total program and grant the money necessary to carry it through.

The love and admiration I bore for my friend, Governor Luther W. Youngdahl, extended far beyond the professional realm. He was a born-again Christian, a committed Lutheran layman of strong religious and political convictions. He was as much at home in the pulpit as he was on the political platform. On Reformation Sunday,

November 2, 1947, he spoke to a large congregation in
New York's Unfinished Cathedral:

> Four hundred and thirty years ago, Martin
> Luther erected three pillars which supported
> the partially destroyed structure of the Church.
> He called for these three:
> 1. The supremacy of the Bible;
> 2. The supremacy of faith;
> 3. The supremacy of the people.
> We must again stress that the Christian
> vocation encompasses all phases of living. We
> need to appreciate the Reformation tradition
> that we are personally responsible for the polit-
> ical conduct of our democracy.

Governor Youngdahl's vital Christian faith and philosophy of personal responsibility never permitted him to
compromise or play politics to gain political goals. As a
younger member of his cabinet, I was a witness to the
moral authority that Youngdahl's commitment to Christ
lent to his office. He was truly a great leader of men.

After two years of gratifying success, everything blew
up. "Youth Commits Suicide at Reformatory," screamed
the headlines. This tragic story was soon followed by
"Buried Bodies Found at St. Cloud." That guards had
killed the prisoners and buried them in the yard before
I came to Minnesota did not deter either the press or the
Governor's political enemies from demanding an investigation by committees of the state legislature. Only days
before this storm broke across the state, I had presented
an enlarged budget to the legislature. I had fully expected
to get the go-ahead to push forward on the three new
projects: expansion of our diagnostic and clinical treatment centers, enlargement statewide of probation and

parole services, and construction of two new forestry camps in northern Minnesota. Now, despite Governor Youngdahl's masterful efforts to help quell the storm, the program lay in apparent ruin.

Following hard on the heels of this debacle came another of a very different kind. Because of my background in criminology and behavioral studies, I had never up to this point in my life been able to understand the Christian doctrine of sanctification. As the leader of the young married couples class in Minneapolis's First Church of the Nazarene, I now found myself faced with having to *teach* it; it was the specified subject for the next quarter. Only because of my excellent teacher training at Pasadena College did I make it (or perhaps fake it) through the first lesson, and then the second. By the third lesson I was floundering. "Experiencing Heart Holiness" was the subject. It convicted me. Before that large class of expectant and trusting couples I felt naked, exposed. The hour seemed endless as I attempted to explain a sanctification I had never experienced. At the close of the class, bathed in sweat and embarrassed over my total failure, I hurried from the room.

In the car on the way home, I poured out my heart to Lois. Never again would I face that class, or any other, until I had experienced what I was preaching. No more church offices or positions of leadership. I felt that I was a fraud before those who trusted and respected me. Without answers, drained and dejected, I drove slowly homeward.

Monday morning broke cold, damp, and cloudy for mid-May. As I climbed into my car and headed for my office, I felt that I carried the entire State of Minnesota on my back. After a few miles, that burden became unbearable. I turned my car off the highway just opposite the Wold-Chamberlain Airport, and there, oblivious to speeding autos and the roar of jet engines, I broke into sobs as I begged God for relief for my convicted heart. All my life, up to that hour, I had felt there was nothing that George Reed couldn't handle. Now all the illusions were swept away. *My* program, *my* hopes, *my* dreams, the best that *my* ingenuity could devise—all were on the verge of being wiped out.

But far more important than all this was the aching void in my heart that must be filled lest I die. I told God that if He would cleanse my proud, self-centered heart and give me the assurance of His Holy Spirit as Comforter, I would do His will and serve Him unreservedly in any way and in any capacity in which He might lead. My professional pride was placed on God's altar and my future at His disposal.

Time passed. It must have been after some two hours spent in tears of repentance and struggle that a still, small voice spoke. "Why don't you let me take full charge of your life?" My instant reply was, "Yes, Lord, I surrender George Reed and his future to You from this hour and forever."

Immediately the heavy burden lifted. It was as if I had awakened at last and sensed with a surge of joy that the Holy Spirit had truly taken full residence in the throne room of my heart. I began to laugh and to praise God. From that moment I knew that God through His Holy Spirit had become my "Senior Partner" for life.

That day God gave me Psalm 75, verses 6 and 7: "For promotion cometh neither from the east, nor from the west, nor from the south. But God is the Judge: He putteth down one and setteth up another." Suddenly God's plan became crystal clear: If advancement came from God and not from man, I determined and contracted with Him that from that day forward I would fear and serve God always, and *fear no man*.

The contract of partnership established that day has never been broken. When a man dares to trust God, he loses his fear of men no matter how great their power or position. I knew that my contribution to this partnership must be a cleansed heart, an ear tuned to the Holy Spirit's direction, and a willingness to move at His prompting. In the years ahead I would many times be severely tested, but my Senior Partner never failed to see me through.

Just days later the Senate Judiciary Committee completed its investigation, and I again presented our expanded budget to the House Appropriations Committee. This time there was no anxiety as I awaited their response and hardly a sense of surprise when it came: We were granted every cent of our budget! It was the go-ahead to expand the Minnesota Youth Conservation Program far beyond my fondest expectations.

The media quickly reversed itself. The Ford Foundation TV series, "The People Act," featured our program on a nationwide one-hour special, while *The Saturday Evening Post, Colliers,* and other publications carried articles that helped our work gain national recognition. From despair and disarray to this! I knew that total surrender to my Partner's leadership had been worth the pain of that struggle.

In the summer of 1951, in the middle of a very successful third term, Governor Youngdahl dropped a bombshell. He had accepted an appointment by President Truman as Federal District Court Judge for the District of Columbia. His decision jolted the people of Minnesota. Many were disappointed that he would pull out in the middle of his unfinished fight for good government. That battle had taken its toll physically, however, and it was on his doctor's advice that he was dropping out of the governorship to take on the less demanding post in

Washington. I understood, but I felt I was losing not only a staunch supporter but a dear personal friend.

The next two years saw the Y.C.C. continue to expand with the full support of Governor Elmer Anderson. Favorable budgets allowed the development of facilities and programs that resulted in a 20 to 30 percent increase in the rehabilitation rate for juvenile and youthful offenders. Those were exciting days as we moved forward in bringing into full operation the new penology for Minnesota's children and youths.

I was having breakfast with friends at the Curtis Hotel on Easter weekend, 1953, when out from an adjoining room walked Federal Judge Luther W. Youngdahl. The words hardly registered as he held out his hand: "George, you'll soon be joining me in Washington to help launch the new Federal Youth Correction Program." It wasn't a question. Neither did I feel inclined to argue. When I regained my composure, I assured him I would send him my vita sheet.

Youngdahl was in a hurry. "You'll be hearing from the Attorney General soon," he assured me, and with a "Happy Easter" to everyone at the table he was gone.

Weeks went by with no word. Our summer vacation plan was to drive to California to visit our families. We went, happy to be going "home," but still wondering about that encounter at the Curtis Hotel. Had it been motivated merely by a momentary enthusiasm for an old friendship? We made a leisurely return over the Rocky Mountains and through Estes Park and then home.

At an early hour the next morning the phone rang. "You were supposed to have seen the President *yesterday* afternoon," the excited voice of my old friend Whit Day announced. A quick call to the Deputy Attorney General confirmed it all. I was to report to Washington within 48 hours.

8

Appointment by Ike

Trust in the Lord with all thine heart, and
lean not unto thine own understanding. In all
thy ways acknowledge Him, and He shall direct
thy paths.

Streaks of light were creeping hesitantly across the
murky sky as my plane circled low over Washington D.C.
early that May morning in 1953. Barely visible were the
monuments to the principles upon which our founding
fathers had established this great nation. There was a
serenity to the panorama from a few thousand feet up
which belied the movement and energy and pulsating
urgency behind the graceful facades of the Capitol. It was
good for a few moments to have a detached view to see
the broader perspective. What transpired here affected
not only every American, but virtually every man,
woman, and child throughout the four corners of the
globe. We had proudly declared our nation to be founded
upon principles of civil and religious liberty. Not only

our own people, but the world itself, so recently wracked by the holocaust of war, held us accountable for that promise.

Emma Willard, American pioneer in women's education and author of several textbooks in use in the early 1880's including her highly acclaimed *Universal History*, desired to show the virtues which "exalt nations and the devices which destroy them." Aptly expressing the conviction of the times she wrote:

> The government of the United States is acknowledged by the wise and good of other nations to be the most free, impartial, and righteous government of the world; but all agree that for such a government to be sustained many years, the principles of truth and righteousness taught in the Holy Scriptures must be practised. *The rulers must govern in the fear of God, and the people obey the laws.*

In his great oration upon the completion of Bunker Hill Monument in 1843, Daniel Webster had thrilled and challenged the people of his day:

> To him who denies or doubts whether our fervid liberty can be combined with law, with order, with the security of property, with the pursuits and advancement of happiness; to him who denies that our forms of government are capable of producing exaltation of soul, and the passion of true glory; to him who denies that we have contributed anything to the stock of great lessons and great examples;—to all these I reply by pointing to [George] Washington! . . .
> But let us remember that we have duties and

obligations to perform, corresponding to the blessings which we enjoy. Let us remember the trust, the sacred trust, attaching to the rich inheritance which we have received from our fathers. Let us feel our personal responsibility, to the full extent of our power and influence, for the preservation of the principles of civil and religious liberty. And let us remember that it is only religion, and morals, and knowledge, that can make men respectable and happy, under any form of government. Let us hold fast the great truth, that communities are responsible, as well as individuals; that no government is respectable, which is not just; that without unspotted purity of public faith, without sacred public principle, fidelity, and honor, no mere forms of government, no machinery of laws, can give dignity to political society.

The Washington Monument, the Lincoln Memorial, the glistening curve of the Potomac—all melted into the horizon on our final swift descent to a bumpy landing at National Airport. Reality engulfed me. I was here to keep faith with Washington and Webster and Willard and the host of others who, with prayer and faith and foresight, had set out to establish "a more perfect union."

After checking in at my hotel, I took a cab directly to the Department of Justice, where I reported to John Lindsey, the Attorney General's administrative assistant. My immediate impression of this obviously bright young lawyer was favorable. Of course, I had no inkling of his ambitions, much less that he would one day become Mayor of New York City. Everything I saw in John Lindsey affirmed my high regard for Eisenhower's administration. A man of tremendous personal charm and charisma, Lindsey had an extraordinary talent for making one feel both at ease and important. During our brief get-acquainted chat, he treated me as though I were already a vital member of the team. Then he took me down the hall and introduced me to Deputy Attorney General William P. Rogers.

Sitting in the Deputy Attorney General's spacious office, I found myself facing a very handsome, immaculately groomed man. I had a momentary vision of him playing the urbane professional in a Hollywood movie. A graduate of Colgate with a law degree from Cornell, and highly regarded by judges and the legal profession across the country, Rogers was a brilliant lawyer with an enviable reputation. That first meeting was destined to be the beginning of a firm friendship which lasted without interruption during our many years together in Washington. As we discussed judicial reform, I sensed that the basic moral principles he expressed, like mine, were derived from faith in the God of the Bible. It was another positive affirmation of the administration I had been called into Washington to join—provided I passed Ike's scrutiny.

We went right to work at that first meeting, doing a great deal of planning that would be implemented in the coming months. I was being brought in as Chairman of the Federal Youth Corrections Division of the United States Board of Parole. I would also be a member of that board and its Vice Chairman, which meant that I was being groomed to become the next Chairman. We spent an hour talking about the new administration's concern for improving the Federal Criminal Justice System and especially about the reforms that were needed in handling juveniles and youth offenders. The lack of physical separation between federal juvenile offenders and hardened criminals was one of the major problems at that time. Special facilities were needed, but it would take six to nine months to acquire and staff them. Preliminary plans were laid for a new approach to Congress that would eliminate the antagonism left over from the Truman era. It had to be done right this time. Rogers also laid out the qualifications of the other new appointees and asked how I felt they would fit into the program.

It seemed as though we had only begun our discussion when word came that Attorney General Herbert Brownell, Jr., was ready to see me. A very wealthy man, Brownell had been the head of a prestigious New York law firm and Chairman of the Republican National Committee that had brought President Eisenhower into the White House. His expansive office was more impressive than anything I had expected, but within a few minutes, in spite of his direct approach and searching questions, he had put me at my ease.

"What do you have to sell?" The question was abrupt, jolting.

"A whole package of reforms . . . that will work . . . and are needed," I responded, caught a bit off guard. Was I trying to *sell* something? Perhaps that was the most forthright way of putting it. The program I had in mind would cost something, and Congress would have to be convinced that it was both necessary and worth the money.

"What qualifies you to be the quarterback of this team?" he cut in as I was adding further explanations about what I had to "sell." Obviously he was measuring his man, testing, probing.

I launched into a brief resume of my record in California and Minnesota, the reforms we had initiated and the success we had achieved. Before I could finish, he interrupted. Obviously he knew my record, or I wouldn't have been there. "Judge Youngdahl either has absolute confidence in you," he said with a smile, "or he has tremendous talent at propagandizing your abilities."

With a wave of his hand, he indicated that he was satisfied with my qualifications and wanted to get down to the immediate business. In the brief discussion that followed concerning the desired reforms in criminal justice that I was expected to oversee and implement, his personal warmth became increasingly evident as the conversation proceeded. I not only felt comfortable with this important man, but I knew that I could trust him completely; he would stand behind me and support me all the way on every part of the program we were discussing. Abruptly our talk came to an end, with his reminder that I was to be back in his office before 10:00 the next morning for a briefing on protocol before we went in to see President Eisenhower.

That evening, after dinner at my hotel, I walked slowly down 16th Street to Pennsylvania Avenue. In a thoughtful mood, I stood outside the tall iron fence surrounding the home of the President. In the distance, beyond the manicured lawn, sparkling fountains, and brilliant flowers, the White House shone like a jewel under the bright glare of floodlights. Solitary, guarded, remote, it reminded me that the President's job was a lonely one and that the responsibilities were almost beyond imagination. Embossed in gold on the fireplace in the State Dining Room, these words had been left by John Quincy Adams for posterity to ponder: "This is the home of the Presidents—may no unworthy man ever abide under its roof."

I thought of the Christian heritage of this nation and how the faith in God that meant so much to its founders was being attacked and displaced. Standing there alone that night, I cried out to God to help Eisenhower and his staff to give America the moral and spiritual leadership she needed—and I asked Him to be my helper and guide when I visited the President the next morning. How I wanted to rise to the challenge to become a vital part of whatever God could do for our nation through the new leadership in Washington!

As I prayed, a still, small voice seemed to whisper the familiar words: "Fear no man!" A quiet calm settled around me as I turned to walk back to my hotel. My commission to service in the nation's capital hadn't, after all, come from the Attorney General of the United States. With the confidence that my Senior Partner was indeed in control, I settled down that night to a much-needed and refreshing sleep.

After a briefing on protocol in Attorney General Herbert Brownell's splendidly appointed office at the Justice Department the next morning, he and I descended in his private elevator from his fifth-floor office into the basement, where his black Cadillac limousine was waiting for us. With an FBI Agent at the wheel, we drove to the White House. Sitting in the backseat (surrounded by bulletproof glass) and looking out through the windshield at the American flag flapping above the right front fender and the Attorney General's flag waving above the left, I seemed to be in the world's longest car. Secret Service agents saluted as the gates parted and we drove through the West entrance and into the White House grounds. Only as the gates closed behind us did the full sense of the moment overwhelm me. I would soon face the President of the United States. I wondered whether the pounding of my heart was audible within the close confines of the limousine.

Because we were a few minutes early, Mr. Brownell thoughtfully gave me a quick tour of the Cabinet Room, the library, and the briefing rooms on our way to the office of the President's appointment secretary. At exactly 11:15 A.M. the door to the Oval Office opened and appointment secretary Stevens ushered the two of us into the presence of the Chief Executive of the United States.

The President was talking on the phone when we entered, and I had a few brief moments to savor the occasion. This was the five-star general who had been my Commander-in-Chief during World War II. We had called him "Ike" then.

Finishing the call, President Eisenhower came around to greet us, then sat down casually on the front of his great mahogany desk. Immediately he began firing questions about my educational and professional background. As I replied, he continued to flip through a file folder that must have contained my entire history. Despite the mental tension involved in giving a good account of myself in this the most crucial interview of my career, I noted that the President's left leg was swinging back and forth, touching the desk on every fourth count in perfect West Point cadence. Somehow it gave me a point of contact, of identity—and of ease.

"Young man, you come highly recommended by Judge Youngdahl, Senator Ed Thye, and Senator Hubert Humphrey," the President was saying. "Tell me about your philosophy of corrections."

I tried to express briefly and concisely what I believed. When he had heard enough from me to satisfy him, the President expressed his own philosophy very simply. "In your handling of these responsibilities," he said in a very serious and concerned tone, "I think it's fine to parole rehabilitated youthful offenders. But whatever you do, don't endanger the public by releasing dangerous criminals."

I had emphasized my desire to rehabilitate youth

offenders and had outlined the success of our program in California and Minnesota. He was clearly in favor of that. However, I could see that one of his major concerns was to reverse the permissiveness that was turning hardened criminals out into the streets to prey once more upon the innocent public. I nodded my agreement.

"We have to treat each case individually," I replied cautiously, "and dispose of it on its own merits."

Ike seemed to sense my concern that the Board make its own decisions. He looked me in the eye and said very earnestly, "Don't ever allow political pressure to influence a decision! The Board must maintain its independent integrity!"

"I'm pleased to hear you say that," I replied. "I've always practiced that principle."

The expression on his face became extremely grave. Gesturing toward the window, he asked, "Did you see the protesters in black hoods picketing in front of the White House?"

Turning to Mr. Brownell for his confirmation, I nodded and replied, "Yes, we did. There must have been about a hundred of them out there when we drove in."

"They're protesting the Rosenbergs' death sentence," he explained. In very somber and measured tones he summarized the evidence upon which the courts had convicted Ethel and Julius Rosenberg of selling to Russia the device for triggering atomic bombs. The Supreme Court had upheld their conviction, and the date of execution had been set. Pressure from liberal quarters was mounting for the President to save them from the electric chair. "I have one of the most difficult decisions of my life to make concerning the pending execution of the Rosenbergs. I'd like to have your thoughts."

"Mr. President," I stammered, surprised by his request, "all I know about the Rosenberg case is what I've read in the papers. I'm not qualified at this time to offer any suggestions. But if you wish, I'll study the case and come up with an opinion."

"I'd appreciate that," he replied quietly. His tone and the expression in his eyes reminded me of the brief vigil I'd had in the front of the White House the evening before. Now I knew that the loneliness I had sensed from beyond the fence was more profound than anything I could imagine.

I thought of the historic decisions this man had made as Commander-in-Chief of the Allied Forces. The burden of that final order to send thousands of brave men to certain death on the beaches of Normandy in that all-out attack on Hitler's fortifications had rested upon these same shoulders. Yet he had just said that the decision he now wrestled with involving the lives of two convicted traitors was as awesome as anything he had faced in the past. Clearly he was thinking not only of the Rosenbergs, but of the possible impact that this decision could have upon other Americans who might be tempted by the promise of financial reward to jeopardize their country's security and thereby place untold millions of people in danger of a third world war. I knew that I was in the presence not only of a great leader, but of a very humble and unassuming man, a man who carried without fanfare or pretext the overwhelming weight of his high office and all its tremendous responsibilities.

Abruptly the President stood to his feet, signaling the end of our meeting. As I arose and he shook my hand in farewell, he looked me in the eye again and said, "Young man, as you assume your new duties of leadership for the U.S. Board of Parole, do not put the public at risk by releasing dangerous persons. Keep your program out of politics and keep the Board of Parole as clean

as a hound's tooth!'' He paused for a moment to empha-
size what he had just said, then concluded: "If I can ever
be of any assistance to you in developing your program,
please let me know. I will want a progress report from
time to time.''

As we said, "Good day, Mr. President,'' and walked
into the outer office, I noted that we had overstayed our
15-minute appointment by ten mintues. The Great Seal
of the President was fixed to the wall directly in front
of me. Suddenly the full impact of that 25 minutes with
Ike hit me. The President was going to nominate me as
a member of the Board of Parole! I knew it was God's
will. This was part of His plan. I thanked Him silently
and renewed my pledge to be His obedient servant as He
continued to guide my steps. As long as I was in His
hands, I had cause to fear nothing and no one.

"Free the Rosenbergs! Free the Rosenbergs!'' The
repeated cry rose from 100 black-clad and hooded
protesters as the Attorney General's limousine carried us
past their waving signs. They were marching back and
forth along the sidewalk outside the fence, where I had
stood with churning emotions the night before. As the
limousine carried us down Pennsylvania Avenue and the
sounds of chanting died away in the distance, I wondered
whether some of them really believed that the Rosenbergs
were innocent, in spite of the evidence that had convinced the court. Perhaps some of the demonstrators
were only registering their disapproval of the death
penalty. I was sure that many of them sincerely believed
that the Soviet Union had peaceful intentions and that
by giving them the atomic bomb and thus depriving the
United States of an overwhelming military advantage, the
cause of world peace had been served. I groped unsuc-
cessfully to understand how any American citizen could

really believe this if he knew anything of the tens of millions of people that Lenin, Stalin, and their successors had murdered. Indeed, the utter disregard for human life in pursuing the goals of international Communism, as fully attested by the record, would have to be part of the framework within which I studied the case.

In view of the stark contrast between the United States and the Soviet Union, there was one particular element of Communism that fascinated me. It was common knowledge that atheism, with its militant goal of stamping out all belief in God, was at the very root of Marxism. Lenin had vowed to close every church and destroy religion completely. The fact that he and his successors had failed and had found it necessary to allow a few churches to remain open in order to placate the masses and to deceive Western tourists with lies about "religious liberty" was no indication that the foundation and intent of Communism had changed in the least. Lenin had declared that belief in God was "the most dangerous abomination, the most loathsome pestilence." In attempting to destroy all religion, however, Lenin had only succeeded in founding another religion, this one based upon faith in the theory that there was no God. And from its very inception, the religion of Marxism had been violently intolerant of any rival faith. The state controlled minds, was intolerant of the slightest dissent, and sealed borders to prevent citizens from escaping the Communist "paradise." No protest such as I had just witnessed outside the White House would be tolerated for one moment on Red Square or anywhere else in Russia!

In contrast, America, founded upon faith in a just God who had created all men with equal rights, was known as the land of liberty. It was not difficult to understand the fundamental basis of disagreement between these two great countries. Nor could it be explained as coincidence that the United States was the one nation with the power to frustrate international Communism's goal of world domination. Her Founding Fathers' faith in God had made the United States the greatest nation on earth. That faith was now under attack as never before, not so much from without as at the hands of well-meaning liberals from within, who were undermining the very foundation of the liberties, justice, and prosperity we enjoyed. I trembled for my country should their attacks upon the faith of our Fathers succeed in removing God from our institutions of government and public life. No longer would an escape to the United States be the dream of millions who suffered under totalitarianism behind Iron and Bamboo Curtains and who longed for the freedoms that U.S. citizens took for granted. Such were the thoughts aroused by the sight of those demonstrators. Sitting in the back of that limousine as we returned to the Department of Justice, I determined anew to defend at all cost the liberty and justice that God desired all men to enjoy without partiality.

My years in public life had already convinced me that if the declaration of our trust in and dependence upon Almighty God ceased to be a meaningful part of our public institutions and leadership, then this nation would perish. This living faith could only be maintained through a strong moral and spiritual leadership, beginning with the President and his Cabinet and carrying on down to all levels of government. It seemed evident that this was the intention of the Founders of these United States.

President Eisenhower seemed to have come to this firm conviction after entering the White House. According to Dr. Edward Elson, Pastor of the National Presbyterian Church in Washington D.C. and Chaplain of the Senate, Ike had been the only President to become a "born-again" Christian during his term of office. Dr. Elson baptized

him in a private ceremony, and the bench on which Ike
kneeled for that occasion is now on display in the Chapel
of Presidents.

The Eisenhower presidency brought a renewed sense
of security and direction that was felt by the average
citizen all across the nation. There were several reasons
for this. We had won World War II, and now the United
States had as its President the five-star general who had
been the wartime Commander-in-Chief of the Allied
Forces in their smashing defeat of Hitler and Mussolini.
Ike had been able to pull hundreds of thousands of fighting men from many nations together and forge them into
the greatest army the world had ever seen. To do this,
he had molded together a huge staff containing dozens
of rival generals—jealous of one another and with
opposing ideas—and had swept to victory. Clearly, most
Americans thought that such a man would make a good
president.

When Ike promised in his campaign that if elected he
would fly to South Korea and settle the war, the American
voters believed him. So did the Communists. They
believed him, too, after he was elected, when he threatened to use the atomic bomb if the Chinese and North
Vietnamese didn't sit down to peace talks. Under that
threat, the 39th parallel was agreed upon as the division
between North and South Korea and hostilities ceased,
at least openly. The Rosenbergs had now effectively taken
that nuclear advantage away from future presidents. This
was the great burden that was weighing so heavily upon
Eisenhower.

There was another weapon, however, even more
powerful and effective, that could never be taken from
us: our faith in God and recourse to Him in prayer. We
could, of course, give up this spiritual weapon or simply
neglect to use it. That was also a great concern to Ike.

He set the example by his own declaration of faith in God, a faith which carried over into every area of his life. He even had Dr. Elson hold a dedication service in the new home he built at Gettysburg before his family moved in.

For my own part, I was very mindful of the principle of separation between church and state and agreed with it wholeheartedly. Church affairs and denominational loyalties should be kept strictly out of business and politics. However, there was no *establishment* of church or religion when a nation through its leaders and institutions openly honored God and admitted its total dependence upon Him. Congress still opened its sessions with prayer "to Almighty God," and our legal tender still had written upon it, "In God we trust."

Such phrases, however, were only empty symbols left over from the faith of our forefathers, unless we constantly reaffirmed that faith in word and deed in everyday life. Personal faith in God could not help but affect everything one said and did, and should make the man or woman of faith a far better public servant than he or she otherwise would be. As I moved into my new responsibilities, it became my continual prayer that God would help me to fulfill the purpose for which He had given me this appointment under President Eisenhower.

9
Life and Death

I have set before you life and death, blessing
and cursing: therefore choose life, that both
thou and thy seed may live: that thou mayest
love the Lord your God, and that thou mayest
obey his voice, and that thou mayest cleave
unto him: for the Lord is your life.

From the very beginning, it had been referred to as the
spy case of the century. Even before they met and
married, the lives of the principals, Julius Rosenberg and
Ethel Greenglass, had followed remarkably similar paths.
They had both grown up in circumstances of poverty,
childhood illness, and deprivation in the same New York
slum neighborhood. Aroused by the suffering and injus-
tice of the 1930's depression era and their own personal
disappointments, both joined radical groups, which were
proliferating at a great rate in those days. Everything from
unemployment and breadlines to the foreclosure of farms
was blamed by the disenchanted upon capitalism and the
monopoly enjoyed by newspapers and industrial giants.

The conspirators-to-be first met at a New Year's Eve fund-raising party for the International Seamen's Union. Ethel was singing on stage. Julius was in the audience. Weekends he was selling subscriptions to *The Daily Worker* door-to-door and leading a Communist group at New York City College. She was a radical union worker, effectively engaged in the "struggle of the working class" against capitalism. After their marriage, they together became more deeply involved with the Communist party: participating in lengthy cell meetings, passing out leaflets, selling *The Daily Worker*, and collecting donations door-to-door. Convinced that capitalism had to be destroyed and the world converted to Communism, by force if necessary, they recruited others to the cause.

Of course they admired the Soviet Union as the leader of world Communism. To become more effectively involved in this international struggle, the Rosenbergs withdrew from open participation with Communism in America and moved their activities underground. It was not soon enough to save Julius's job, however. Military intelligence had already become alarmed by their affiliations and activities, and as a result Julius was fired from his position as a civilian junior engineer with the United States Army Signal Corps in Brooklyn. Thereafter it was much more difficult to trace their activities. They saw less and less of former friends, and their lives took on an air of mystery. Julius worked his way up through various levels of responsibility in the Communist underground, until he became the leader of a spy ring that supplied the Soviet Union with American military secrets. The alleged motive? To advance international Communism, which in the end would turn the United States, the country they loved, into a proletarian paradise.

Julius and Ethel had not acted alone. Other members of the ring included Ethel's brother and sister-in-law,

David and Ruth Greenglass, and Morton Sobell and Max Elitcher. Both of the latter had been involved with Julius Rosenberg in Communist activities as far back as New York City College days. Sobell and Elitcher gave Rosenberg U.S. Navy secrets, particularly relating to gunfire control. Greenglass supplied his brother-in-law with atomic bomb secrets. Rosenberg passed the classified information on to the Soviet Union through higher connections, a part of the conspiracy which was never uncovered by the FBI.

When two other members of the ring, Dr. Fuchs and Harry Gold, were arrested, Sobell fled with his family to Mexico, where he lived under various aliases until he was captured and returned to the United States by Mexican authorities. Rosenberg had urged David and Ruth Greenglass to flee to Mexico too, but it was too late. They were also caught in the net. Ruth was never indicted, but eventually David Greenglass and Max Elitcher made a full confession and implicated Julius and Ethel Rosenberg and Morton Sobell. These were the basic facts turned up in the investigation and established by the lengthy trial.

Pleading the Fifth Amendment in the witness stand whenever they were questioned about their Communist Party membership and activities, the Rosenbergs insisted they were innocent. They denied every charge against them. Since much of the government's case rested upon the testimony of Greenglass and Elitcher, defense attorneys tried their best to discredit them. Emmanuel Bloch, who teamed with his father, Alexander Bloch, to defend the Rosenbergs, reminded the jury that David Greenglass was a "self-confessed espionage agent" who "swore to support our country . . . when he entered the army" and thereafter "disgraced the uniform of every soldier in the United States by his actions." Worse than that, he had tried to destroy his sister, Ethel, and her husband in order to save his own skin. Bloch argued persuasively that the testimony of such a man couldn't be trusted. In Bloch's words:

> . . . I don't think that there is a word in the English vocabulary or in the dictionary of any civilization which can describe a character like Dave Greenglass. . . . Any man who will testify against his own blood and flesh, his own sister, is repulsive, is revolting. . . the lowest of lowest animals. . . .
>
> This is not a man; this is an animal. . . . Did you look at him [in the witness stand]? . . . He smirked and he smiled. . . . Maybe some people enjoy lynchings. . . have you ever come across a man, who comes around to bury his own sister and smiles!
>
> Tell me, is this the kind of a man you are going to believe? . . . What kind of a man can we disbelieve if we are going to believe Dave Greenglass? . . . Come on, be honest with yourselves, ladies and gentlemen. Is that the kind of testimony that you are going to accept?

One of Sobell's attorneys, Edward Kuntz, who had a voice like thunder and had to be cautioned by Federal Judge Irving R. Kauffman that his confidential whispers to his client were so loud that they disturbed the court, tore into the credibility of Elitcher like a tiger. He told the jury that Elitcher was a miserable liar and perjurer (he had admitted perjuring himself on a job application), "who will kill another man to save his own miserable skin." He reasoned that Elitcher, caught in a trap, had made a deal with the government to feather his own nest. And even then, according to Kuntz, Elitcher's testimony

was tenuous and unbelievable and had failed to establish
any solid link between Sobell and Rosenberg. Without
Elitcher's testimony, there was no case. Elitcher himself,
Kuntz declared, was a nothing, a man of zero credibility,
ridiculous:

> I saw the most amazing experience in my
> court life in this case. I saw [the government
> attorneys]...all of them, like the mountain,
> they labored and labored and labored, and they
> brought forth a mouse—Elitcher.

The chief prosecuting attorney for the government,
Irving H. Saypol, knew how to deal with these attempts
to discredit his key witnesses. Of course these men were
spies who had betrayed their own country, but at least
they had repented. They had had a change of heart and
admitted the truth, whereas the Rosenbergs had added
"the supreme touch to their betrayal of this country . . . by
lying and lying and lying here brazenly in an attempt to
deceive you, to lie their way out of what they did." He
argued that the testimony of Greenglass was believable
for the very reason that, rather than gaining anything for
him, it incriminated him: "By his own plea of guilty, by
his own voluntary act, without weaving a web of lies in
an attempt to deceive you, he has made himself liable to
the death penalty, too." It wasn't he who destroyed his
sister by telling the truth, but the Rosenbergs who
destroyed him by "dragging an American soldier into the
sordid business of betraying his country for the benefit
of the Soviet Union." In his summation to the jury, Saypol
declared:

> Greenglass' relations toward his older sister, Ethel,
> and her husband, Julius, were such that he was

willing prey to their Communistic propaganda. He committed this crime because they persuaded him to do it. . . .

He has been sentenced to thirty years, the maximum term of imprisonment. He can gain nothing from testifying as he did in this courtroom except the initial relief, the moral satisfaction in his soul of having told the truth and tried to make amends. Harry Gold, who furnished the absolute corroboration of the testimony of the Greenglasses, forged the necessary link in the chain that points indisputably to the guilt of the Rosenbergs.

Not one question was asked of him by any defendant on cross-examination.

The atom bomb secrets stolen by Greenglass at the instigation of the Rosenbergs were delivered by Harry Gold right into the hands of an official representative of the Soviet Union. The veracity of David and Ruth Greenglass and of Harry Gold is established by documentary evidence and cannot be contradicted. . . . Max Elitcher, the testimony of Harry Gold, the registration card, the bank account. . .the testimony of Dr. Bernhardt. . .proves beyond any doubt the verity of what the Greenglasses have sworn to in this courtroom.

The cost of the truth and his testimony to Elitcher was the ruination of his reputation. He lost his job. He has admitted he had been a Communist and that he had been recruited into this Soviet espionage ring by Sobell and by Rosenberg. . . .

Greenglass is a confessed spy and Elitcher has admitted that some years ago he did not disclose his Communist Party membership in an application; but these men under the greatest stress have stood up here and disclosed the truth about their past activities. They have not compounded their sins by trying to lie to you here in this courtroom. . . .

While Rosenberg attacks the Greenglasses today, seven years ago it was the Rosenbergs who took this same David Greenglass and set him to betraying his country. It was Sobell, at Rosenberg's instigation, who recruited Elitcher. These witnesses were not your choice, nor were they mine . . . they were selected by these defendants as their associates and partners in crime. . . .

We have not only the testimony of Ruth and David Greenglass about Rosenberg's espionage activities. We have Elitcher's . . . Harry Gold . . . the bank account, the wrapping paper, the testimony of Dr. Bernhardt, Dorothy Abel, Evelyn Cox, of Schneider, who took the passport pictures. . . . The evidence as to the Rosenbergs' guilt is incontrovertible . . . established by the proof, not beyond a reasonable doubt, but beyond any conceivable doubt.

The testimony and evidence presented by the government in its case against the defendants was enough to convince the jury, which deliberated only six hours in reaching its verdict. On March 29, 1951, climaxing a sensational three-week trial that had stirred up a storm around the world, both Rosenbergs were found guilty of conspiracy to commit wartime espionage. The jury made no recommendation for mercy, nor did Judge Kauffman. The Judge described the defendants' crime as "worse than murder" and "a sordid, dirty business not to be compared with Nathan Hale's sacrifice of his life for his country." On April 5, 1951, Judge Kauffman sentenced Julius Rosenberg and his wife, Ethel, to death for the treasonable act of passing atomic bomb secrets to

Soviet agents. Their accomplice, Morton Sobell, received 30 years in prison. David Greenglass's sentence was reduced to 15 years because he had turned State's evidence against his sister and brother-in-law and the other co-defendants.

It was of particular interest to me, as I read the record, that the Judge, in his comments, remarked upon "the denial of God" that lies at the heart of Communism, and equated that with "denial of the sanctity of the individual" and loss of liberty. This certainly agreed with the faith upon which this country had been founded, a faith that was affirmed in public schools when I was a boy, but which was now being explicitly denied on all fronts. Addressing the Court, and then the Rosenbergs, Judge Kauffman declared:

> It is ironic that the very country which these defendants betrayed and sought to destroy placed every safeguard around them for obtaining a fair and impartial trial, a trial which consumed three weeks in this court.
>
> I recall the defendant, Julius Rosenberg, testifying that our American system of jurisprudence met with his approval and was preferred over Russian justice. Even the defendants realized by this admission that this type of trial would not have been offered to them in Russia.
>
> Certainly for a Russian national accused of a conspiracy to destroy Russia, not one day would have been consumed in a trial. Yet they made a choice of devoting themselves to the Russian ideology of denial of God, denial of the sanctity of the individual and aggression against free men everywhere, instead of serving the cause of liberty and freedom.

Your crime is worse than murder. Plain, deliberate, contemplated murder is dwarfed in magnitude by comparison with the crime you have committed. Your offense has given the Russians the atom bomb years before our best scientists predicted Russia would perfect the bomb; and has already caused the Communist aggression in Korea, with the resultant casualties exceeding 50,000 Americans; and who knows but that millions more of innocent people may pay the price of your treason. Indeed, by your betrayal, you undoubtedly have altered the course of history to the disadvantage of our country!

My study of the case convinced me that money had not been the predominant motive. Julius Rosenberg apparently had believed, in spite of the millions of people they had murdered and the totalitarian regimes they established, that the Communists had the answers to the world's problems. This was primarily why he had aided the Soviets, although the defendants also received some cash for the betrayal of their country. To the very end, the Rosenbergs' loyalty to the Soviets remained even stronger than their own natural instinct of self-preservation. The defendants might have been able to avoid the death penalty if they had been willing to cooperate.

This attitude is particularly difficult to understand in view of the Rosenbergs' own admission that an open, fair trial such as theirs would have been impossible in the Soviet Union. Apparently they believed the argument that terror and oppression were still necessary in the Soviet Union and other Communist countries, because the true benefits of Marxism-Leninism would only be realized when Communism had taken over the entire world.

Therefore, the end justified the means: The "paradise" that Communism supposedly would produce when it had complete control everywhere justified imposing it upon the entire world, no matter the cost in deceit, brutality, and bloodshed.

Before sentencing the Rosenbergs to death, Judge Kauffman spoke these solemn words. They bear repeating:

> I can only conclude that the defendants entered into this most serious conspiracy against their country with full realization of its implications. I feel that I must pass such sentence upon the principals in this diabolical conspiracy to destroy a God-fearing nation, which will demonstrate with finality that this nation's security must remain inviolate; that traffic in military secrets, whether promoted by slavish devotion to a foreign ideology or by a desire for monetary gain, must cease.
>
> The evidence indicated quite clearly that Julius Rosenberg was the prime mover in this conspiracy. However, let no mistake be made about the role which his wife, Ethel Rosenberg, played in the conspiracy. Instead of deterring him from pursuing his ignoble cause, she encouraged and assisted the cause.
>
> What I am about to do is not easy for me. I have deliberated for hours, days, and nights. I have carefully weighed the evidence. Every nerve, every fiber of my body has been taxed. I am just as human as are the people who have given me the power to impose sentence. I am convinced beyond any doubt of your guilt. I have searched the records; I have searched the

statutes; and I cannot violate the solemn and sacred trust that the people of this land have placed in my hands were I to show leniency to the defendants Rosenberg.

It is not in my power, Julius and Ethel Rosenberg, to forgive you. Only the Lord can find mercy for what you have done.

The sentence of the court upon Julius and Ethel Rosenberg is that for their crime they are sentenced to death. The sentence will be executed according to law in the week beginning on Monday, May 21.

The Rosenbergs' attorneys, Emmanuel and Alexander Bloch, desperately pursued every avenue of possible appeal. Their only success was to delay briefly the execution, which the government was determined to accomplish as quickly as possible. On May 25, 1953, the Supreme Court, refusing for the third time to grant a hearing to Julius and Ethel Rosenberg, directed the U.S. Court of Appeals in New York to vacate its stay of execution order, granted in February. Seven justices favored denying any hearing to the Rosenbergs, while two justices— Hugo L. Black and William O. Douglas—took the position that their cases should be reviewed by the Supreme Court. The Court's action resulted in an order to Judge Kauffman to set a new execution date.

The progress of the case and the appeals process were being followed around the world as no other trial of the century. The Communists had most to gain and mounted a well-organized international campaign to deny that the Rosenbergs had ever been agents of the Soviets and to denounce capitalism and the American judicial process. Many distinguished non-Communists—Professor Albert Einstein, the President of France, and Pope Pius XII

among others—added their voices to the worldwide outcry protesting the pending execution. United States
embassies in foreign countries were attacked by outraged
mobs. Religious groups argued against the death penalty
on moral and even biblical grounds. Others pleaded for
the Rosenbergs to be spared for the sake of their two
young sons. As I gave my attention to the protests and
appeals as well as to the facts, I began to gain a small
insight into the pressure that Eisenhower must have been
feeling.

In reviewing the court records and testimony of our
leading atomic scientists, I became convinced that the
traitorous act of the Rosenbergs had advanced by 10 or
12 years the ability of Communist Russia to manufacture
atomic bombs that could destroy this nation and much
of the world's population. Korea was the last arena where
the United States would ever again be able to bring a
cease-fire by threatening use of nuclear weapons. One
day, as a result of the Rosenbergs' betrayal, our own
nation could face the threat of annihilation by a massive
Soviet nuclear attack and be forced to surrender. That
would bring the worldwide "peace" that the Rosenbergs
told the Greenglasses they were working toward. In view
of the magnitude of their crime, I felt that I had no choice
except to recommend to the President that the course
he had already set was the right one and that he should
stand firm in his resolve to back the courts. But before
I could begin my report to the President, events took a
sudden turn.

Emmanuel Bloch was ecstatic with joy on June 18,
1953, as he informed the Rosenbergs that the Supreme
Court had granted a stay of execution. The very next day,
however, in an unprecedented special session, the High
Court reversed itself, plunging the Blochs, Rosenbergs,
and supporters into despair once again. In that final

decision, on June 19, 1953, the U.S. Supreme Court refused to save Julius and Ethel Rosenberg from death in the electric chair. It upheld the legality of the death sentence imposed by Federal Judge Irving R. Kauffman and scheduled its execution for that night at 11:00 P.M.

Four months earlier, on February 11, 1953, President Eisenhower had refused a first clemency plea, saying that the Rosenbergs' betrayal of the United States atomic secrets to Russia could bring death to "many, many thousands of innocent citizens." And now, less than an hour after the Supreme Court had announced its verdict, President Eisenhower refused executive clemency for the second time. The President explained his decision with these words:

> The execution of two human beings is a grave matter. But even graver is the thought of the millions of dead whose deaths may be directly attributable to what these spies have done.
>
> When in their most solemn judgment, the tribunals of the United States have adjudged them guilty and the sentence is just, I will not intervene in this matter.

In a desperate effort to save the Rosenbergs' lives, their sympathizers bombarded judges at all levels with last-minute petitions. Supreme Court Justices Burton, Black, Frankfurter, and Jackson each received separate motions for a stay and each rejected them. Three separate appeals to stay the execution were presented to Judge Kauffman, who was being closely guarded around the clock by FBI agents. Two separate appeals to the Federal Circuit Court of Appeals in the last hours also failed. Mrs. Sophie Rosenberg, mother of Julius, arrived in Washington D.C., pleading for an audience with the President. He declined to see her. Emmanuel Bloch, who was taking care of the Rosenbergs' children and brought them to the death house for regular visits with their parents, made a last-minute emotion-choked appeal at the White House gate for a chance to speak personally with President Eisenhower. The President denied the request.

The gripping details of that final evening's events were told to me by my friend, the late Edward Donovan, former Corrections Commissioner of New York State, who supervised the execution at Sing Sing Prison. Emmanuel Bloch had received a report that the Attorney General had acquiesced to his appeal to delay the execution until the Jewish Sabbath had passed, thus giving one more day in which to work for a reprieve. When Bloch, calling from Washington, reached Warden Denno by phone to confirm the good news, he was informed that, on the contrary, the execution had been moved forward from 11:00 to 8:00 o'clock that evening. It was 7:30. Only one-half hour to go!

Something snapped in Bloch, and he began to scream and rave almost incoherently against the "animals" who would do something so "barbaric" as to reject his petition "without even hearing us!" Other lawyers looking on tried their best to calm him, but it was almost 8:00 o'clock before Bloch regained control. In a frenzy he again managed to get through to Sing Sing on the phone, this time to U.S. Marshal William A. Carroll. Distraught, he managed to blurt out, "This is Manny. Tell Julie and Ethel . . . I did the best I could for them. Tell them . . . I'll take care of the children. Tell them . . . I love them. Tell them. . . ." The sobs became uncontrollable. Manny dropped the phone and buried his head in his hands.

One of those present in Sing Sing that evening was William R. Conklin. His written report of the controversial execution, which appeared next morning on the front page of *The New York Times*, included the following:

Stoic and tight-lipped to the end, Julius and Ethel Rosenberg paid the death penalty in the electric chair for their wartime atomic espionage for Soviet Russia.

The pair, first husband and wife to pay the supreme penalty here, and the first in the United States to die for espionage, went to their deaths with a composure that astonished all witnesses.

Julius, 35 years old, was first to enter the glaringly-lighted, white-walled death chamber. He walked slowly behind Rabbi Irvin Koslowe, a chaplain at Sing Sing, who was intoning the Twenty-third Psalm, *"The Lord is my shepherd, I shall not want."* As Rosenberg neared the brown-stained oak chair, he seemed to sway from side to side.

Guards quickly placed him in the chair. He was clean-shaven, no longer wearing his mustache, and wore a white t-shirt. At 8 P.M. the first shock of 200 volts, with its ten amperes, coursed through his body. After two subsequent shocks, his life ended at 8:06 P.M. Dr. H. W. Kipp and Dr. George Mc-Cracken applied stethoscopes to his chest, and Dr. Kipp said, "I pronounce this man dead."

Ethel Rosenberg, 37-year-old wife, entered the death chamber a few minutes after the dead body of her husband was removed. She wore a dark green print dress with white polka dots; and like her husband, was shod in loafer-type cloth slippers. Her hair was close cropped on top to permit contact of an electrode. Just before she reached the chair, she held out her hand to a friend.

President Eisenhower, Judge Kauffman, the U.S. Supreme Court, and the entire nation were denounced by some 5000 demonstrators that night in New York City's Union Square in a rally organized by The Committee to Save the Rosenbergs. Calling Eisenhower "bloodthirsty" and worse, Communist speakers harangued the crowd into hysteria. The whole city was like a time bomb about to explode. Police Commissioner George Monaghan, in anticipation of possible rioting, had ordered a citywide alert of the police force.

Protests were even more intense overseas, where millions penned clemency pleas for the condemned pair. Capitalizing on the unpopularity of the death penalty, Communists were able to mount impressive demonstrations against America in many major foreign cities. In Paris, masses of flowers, placed by sympathizers, were banked at the wall of the Tuileries Gardens where Nazis had shot resistance fighters in 1944. The Soviets gained not only from the military secrets they obtained from the Rosenbergs, but from the propaganda they made out of their execution.

There was violence at the funeral. In his eulogy of the dead pair, Emmanuel Bloch, who had become almost totally involved with them and in the care of their children during the three years since their arrest, used rash language. He called the execution of the Rosenbergs "murder" and blamed it on President Eisenhower, Mr. Brownell, and J. Edgar Hoover. Bloch declared that it was "Nazism that killed the Rosenbergs" and blamed American leaders for "irrationality, insanity, barbarism, and murder." He was defending himself against proceedings instituted by the Bar Association of New York to disbar him for these remarks when he died of a heart attack in the bathroom of his apartment a few months later.

Emmanuel Bloch was by no means a Communist, but he became the unwitting and tragic victim of emotions that Communism often exploits to camouflage its evil and serve its own ends. In his passion to save the lives of Julius and Ethel Rosenberg, he seemed to have lost the capacity to think rationally about larger issues. In an editorial of June 23, 1953, *The San Francisco Chronicle* had this to say about his intemperate remarks at the funeral:

> It was not, as he [Bloch] said, " . . . the face of Nazism that killed the Rosenbergs." Between the almost painfully slow processes of justice as demonstrated in the three years of the Rosenberg case, and the loaded "justice" dispensed by Adolf Hitler's courts, there is a breadth of difference that is obvious to every American, certainly to any practicing attorney.
>
> There is room for honest differences of opinion as to whether, in the absolute sense, the Rosenbergs deserved to die for their crime. There is no room for doubt that they were accorded full and fair access to the American judicial process, or that those in authority did what in conscience they felt was right.

Thirty-three years later, the case is still being fought with varying degrees of passion in the hearts of both the well-meaning and the opportunists. The Espionage Act of 1917 itself is a factor. Did its meaning extend to the sale of secrets to an ally, as Russia was at the time? Would the death penalty have been imposed had the recipient of secrets been England—or Israel? The extremity of the sentence is a factor. The death penalty for espionage had never yet been imposed in a civil court. Compassion is a factor. "Don't let my mommy die," pleaded the placards waved high above the heads of the protestors.

I firmly believe, however, that in light of the ever-present and growing danger of an all-out nuclear World

War III that could turn this entire planet into an inferno of total destruction, Judge Kauffman, the Justices of the Supreme Court, and President Eisenhower were jointly justified in ordering the execution of the Rosenbergs. The fairness of the penalty can only be questioned in relation to the fact that other defendants who seemed to be equally culpable were not executed and are out of prison today. The betrayal of atomic secrets by all members of this spy ring is largely responsible for the fact that today the Soviet Union has literally thousands of nuclear missiles aimed at the United States and Western Europe, each warhead many times more powerful than the bomb that destroyed Hiroshima.

In spite of the protests, the prevailing opinion in this country at the time of the trial seemed to be that the Rosenbergs had been treated fairly, and having been found guilty in open court, deserved the sentence that was imposed. In an editorial on March 30, 1951, *The New York Times* expressed it succinctly in words that could apply as well today:

> They [the Rosenbergs] can only be considered, like so many others, as willing victims of the Big Lie which pictures Soviet Russia as a paradise and entices its dupes to regard any means as justified to promote its ends. If this is the explanation, it cannot in any way excuse the culprits or mitigate their crime.

Who could doubt that, with the present realities of the Cold War, our nation is today even more vulnerable to acts of espionage than during the hottest of declared wars? Could this explain why increasing numbers of apparently loyal American citizens have been apprehended recently for selling military secrets to Soviet agents, seemingly for no higher motive than the money they have received in exchange? Perhaps the knowledge that the death penalty is not imposed for espionage in times of "peace" also serves as an encouragement to take what is consequently considered to be a substantially lesser risk. That part of the Rosenberg case—the death penalty—is still an issue of great importance today, as it proved to be throughout my entire career.

10

A New Direction

Give instruction to a wise man, and he will be yet wiser; teach a just man, and he will increase in learning.

Engrossing and time-consuming as my study of the Rosenberg case was, the larger issues of penal reform demanded my immediate attention. It was a legislative decision made in 1950 by the Eighty-First Congress that had catapulted me into a leadership position in Washington D.C., the nerve center of the nation. The Federal Youth Corrections Act of 1950 grew out of Congress's recognition that a more flexible approach to the sentencing and disposition of juveniles was required. It was a milestone in penal reform and in my life as well.

Not until three years later was the new law actually implemented. The blue-ribbon panel of federal judges who had initiated the proceedings insisted that the President appoint to the new Board the nation's most highly qualified men in the fields of criminology, human behavior, and the law. To these men would be given the task of implementing a new departure from the punitive philosophy of dealing with criminals and replacing it with a training and treatment program designed to redirect antisocial behavior. Rehabilitation, not retribution, was to be the new focus.

This, then, was the program which I had been called to Washington to direct. I was very aware of the scrutiny I would be working under—from the President, the Attorney General, the Federal Judiciary, correctional administrators around the nation, and perhaps most of all the thousands of parents of federal youth offenders. They were all looking to me to make this new concept work.

In those days of new beginning, there were times when I felt almost overwhelmed by the heavy responsibility I carried. Philippians 4:13 was my daily reminder and reassurance: "I can do all things through Christ, who strengthens me." Sometimes that affirmation was little more than a claim I clung to with small faith. But the Object of that faith was omnipotent, and He never failed to give the needed help.

On August 5, 1953, I was officially advised by the Attorney General that the new Federal Youth Corrections Division of the U.S. Board of Parole was a fact, and that I was confirmed as its first Chairman. I was shortly joined by Dorothy McCullough Lee and Lewis Grant, both highly qualified lawyers, who rounded out the three-member board. We were in business.

That September I launched out on a whirlwind tour of most of the federal penal institutions and forestry camps. Of these, six east of the Mississippi were designated as youth institutions, and, with the full cooperation of Director James V. Bennett of the Federal Bureau of Prisons, all adult prisoners were transferred to other penal institutions. No longer would federal prisons be a graduate school in crime, where older and more hardened criminals would instruct the juveniles in the finer points of their craft and inspire them with their exploits.

The key to the entire program for youth offenders was the diagnostic center established at Ashland Reformatory in Kentucky. Here, over a span of 90 days, a clinical team subjected each juvenile entering the system to a rigorous diagnostic study covering all aspects of behavioral and emotional problems. Thus we could classify youths into small groups having similar treatment needs.

One of the major thrusts was the testing program which determined the trainable vocational abilities of each youth. The classification committee assigned each individual into the educational and vocational program which could best maximize his talents. The sprawling campus of the Chillicothe Federal Reformatory in Ohio provided vocational training programs unequaled by any public vocational school in the country. Here young men could train in welding, metal shop, auto mechanics, electronics, and airplane mechanics.

The airplane mechanics school became a showpiece. Equipped with a variety of modern aircraft, the school offered a two-year program through which youths with sufficient ability and aptitude could earn an airplane mechanic's certificate. The Federal Government affirmed its confidence in our program by accepting these young men to service both commercial and military aircraft at any airport facility in the country. For the first few years, the number of highly trained airplane mechanics graduating from our school was insufficient to meet the demand.

Youths not suited for vocational training were transferred to the forestry programs in West Virginia, where they developed disciplined work habits, positive attitudes, and improved health. Along with the work program, these young men attended a regular or remedial school geared to their needs. Most earned their high school diplomas. Caseworkers provided an excellent individual counseling program designed to help youths gradually change attitudes and lifestyles.

Three years after its inception, the Federal Youth Corrections Act was certified for the entire nation. To meet the need in the western half of the United States, a second diagnostic center was added, this one in Colorado. Within four years, nine federal institutions and two forestry camps, having an average population of 5550 federal juvenile and youth offenders, had been retooled as "youth institutions."

In 1958, nearly 2000 new inmates were absorbed into the system under the Youth Act. These young offenders served an average of just under 20 months prior to release on parole. It was with considerable pride that we could point to a 65 percent success rate for the juvenile parolees who came out of our federal programs. This compared with the 47.5 percent who were making a satisfactory adjustment in the community on the state level. The record spoke for itself and gained considerable public support for our program.

"Bob" was one of the thousands of young men who made good under the Federal Youth Corrections program. He was only 19 when he pulled a bank robbery. Bob was a streetwise kid but hardly the pro to be tackling this big a job. When the handcuffs closed around his wrists, he knew he had done an incredibly stupid thing and one that he could neither laugh off nor talk his way out of.

This youthful felon had no previous record, but his history was replete with the classic danger signals.

Though above average in intelligence, Bob was two years behind academically. His father had been an alcoholic, and, although not abusive, had aroused an ardent contempt in his son. After a traumatic divorce, the mother had remarried. The stepfather was much that the father was not: He was successful, he enjoyed a respected standing in the community, he established order in the home—and he totally rejected his stepson. Eager to maintain her own security in her new marriage, the mother followed her husband's lead and ignored her son. Hungry for identity, recognition, and success—by any means and at any price—Bob pulled a gun that sunny Friday morning in 1954. He was caught almost immediately.

From the beginning, Bob took Ashland seriously. He finished high school and began training as a technician in the institutional hospital. One year later, by special arrangement, he entered the junior college nearby. Each day he was escorted out for classes and was returned each evening to the security of the federal facility.

After a little more than three years, we were ready to make proof on the outside of Bob's training and his improved understanding of his problems. We all knew, however, that unless the family attitude had changed, we were headed for failure. The local probation officer did a splendid job of laying the groundwork at home. The stepfather surprised us all by taking an active interest in Bob's rehabilitation—and, again, Bob's mother followed her husband's lead.

For the first three months of his parole, Bob worked as a laborer. It was his decision to try to secure employment in one of the area hospitals in an effort to make use of his training. But now his record caught up with him, and those doors of opportunity closed one by one. Bob had reached a crisis point, we knew. Would the old feelings of rejection compound and undo all the progress he had made?

Ironically, it was the stepfather who, in a reversed role, provided the bridge to Bob's restored sense of confidence. He put Bob in touch with a doctor friend who offered him a job as a medical technician.

The story didn't end there. The hospital offered Bob a full scholarship to one of the top medical schools in the country. It was only after he had completed his medical training and was ready to enter practice that we released him from parole supervision. On that day, under the authority of the Federal Youth Corrections Act, Bob was pronounced fully rehabilitated, and an order was signed expunging his conviction from the record. Stories like this could be multiplied, and it was such results that proved the value of the program.

In April of 1956, a second National Conference on Parole convened. The first one had been called by President Roosevelt back in 1939. The intervening years had seen tremendous social changes, and it was now imperative that we reassess the criminal justice system's responses to those changes through the nation's parole boards.

Sweeping, even scathing, attacks on parole were frequently voiced in the thirties and forties. Much of the criticism was understandable. As President Roosevelt had reminded the first conference, less than a dozen of the 46 states then having parole laws had provided the money and personnel necessary to operate.

The 1939 conference's manifesto, *Principles of Parole*, became a bible for the entire spectrum of issues. A major and sensitive point was that, in most cases and in most states, the paroling authorities had before them wholly inadequate data upon which to make parole decisions.

Bad judgments and the resultant public outcry were inevitable.

In 1956, the public's perception of parole was wisely addressed by keynote speaker Chief Justice Earl Warren when he declared: "It would be a very wholesome thing if out of this conference could come a public awareness of the fact that the parole of a prisoner is not an act of coddling but, on the contrary, it is an extension of the State's supervision while he is trying to re-establish himself in society."

Attorney General Brownell aptly placed the two conferences in right perspective when he identified the 1939 meeting as an "outgrowth of public apprehension resulting from either misuse of parole or lack of understanding of parole procedures." Parole in those early days had often been "a source of scandal," he admitted. He then proceeded to set forth the following objectives for the 1956 conference:

1. To elevate existing parole standards and practices;
2. To promulgate and publish manual and guide materials on the best parole principles and practice;
3. To focus nationwide attention on the importance of parole in the control of delinquency and crime.

Mr. Brownell reserved his highest praise for the new Federal Youth Corrections Division of the U.S. Board of Parole:

> Already I am very encouraged by the fine showing made by the youth program. Chairman Reed of the Youth Corrections Division

recently reported that some 40% of all youths
eligible under the Federal Youth Act have during the past year been committed under its
special provisions. The success so far is an
excellent beginning and one that holds great
hope for young federal offenders.

Mr. Brownell's confidence in me, so generously
expressed during that memorable conference, came to
fruition two years later, when President Eisenhower
appointed me Chairman of the United States Board of
Parole. That quasi-judicial body had nationwide authority
to grant, deny, or revoke parole, as it saw fit, to the more
than 28,000 federal prisoners then under its jurisdiction.
Its decisions were unilateral. Once made, they were not
subject to review—either by the courts, the Attorney
General, or the President of the United States. The chairman was not only presiding officer of the U.S. Board of
Parole, and an administrative head within the Department
of Justice, but director of all federal officers supervising
the approximately 15,000 parolees in communities across
the nation.

The time frame in which I stepped into my new post
was unique in the annals of American social history.
Young veterans who had exuberantly, and in some cases
hastily, traded the horrors of war for domestic bliss were
now fathers of teenagers. Many of these parents were
"depression kids" and were determined to spare their
children the hard times they had experienced. The feeling of national security—the sense of belonging to the
strongest, most respected, and most advanced nation on
earth—was heady stuff for young Americans of the fifties. But this euphoria faded as the realities of the Cold
War set in. Backyard bomb shelters, emergency food supplies, and first-aid courses proliferated.

And so did crime. In 1960, more than 785,000 children were referred to police and juvenile courts. During that year alone, crime increased by 18 percent. FBI Director J. Edgar Hoover reported a 98 percent increase in known crime over the prior decade. World War II's war babies were clearly registering a confusing resistance to authority, and none of our much-vaunted advances in the realms of science and technology could compensate for the moral and social malaise which seemed to grip our nation.

Given the hard facts of the escalating crime rate, the mood of the country in general and that of FBI Chief J. Edgar Hoover in particular was not readily amenable to the whole concept of parole: of bringing the federal offender back onto the streets before he had paid his "full debt" to society. I was convinced, however, that bigger prisons and longer sentences were not the whole answer. Incarceration had to be more than a retributive act, and eventual release had to be more than a revolving door through those same hopeless prison walls.

My board and I moved ahead, therefore, on two new and progressive programs. Taking their cue from the provisions of the Federal Youth Corrections program, the federal judges supported the passage of the Adult Indeterminate Sentencing Law. The Parole Board would now have jurisdiction to determine the date of parole eligibility and would order, at the appropriate time, the granting of parole. The U.S. Board of Parole now had full discretion to establish minimum sentences and to release adult prisoners when they had gained the maximum benefit from their institutional experiences.

How did the new sentencing law work? The statistics indicated that during 1960, 35.7 percent of federal prisoners released were granted parole. Approximately one-third had served their full time, minus "good time" credits, and were *mandatory* releases. The remaining one-third were released upon the expiration of their sentences. It was with considerable satisfaction that I could report that over a five-year period under the new law eight out of ten parolees stayed clean after release.

We were learning from experience and careful study. Research revealed that certain types of offenders more often violated parole than others. Auto thieves, for instance, were the worst risks; they violated parole in 34.6 percent of the cases. They were followed closely by writers of fraudulent checks and forgers. White-collar workers, on the other hand, were good risks. Murderers were, statistically, one of the lowest parole violation risks. Perhaps it was the nature of the crime: the moment of passion, the accessibility of a weapon, the reluctance to repeat a long prison experience. Whatever the reasons, we were willing to explore the possibilities a bit more deeply for those parole applicants who came from low-risk groups.

The second program for which Congress allocated funds involved a series of experimental "halfway houses," designed to provide a prerelease experience that would better ease the parolee into community life. It has long been recognized that the period immediately follow-ing release from prison is extremely critical—especially so for the young offender. The shock of reentry from the regimented and protected environment of the institution to a free community is frequently too much for a young offender to handle. The juvenile often faces the same temptations, the same impoverished social climate, the same inadequate home. For these young men, the pre-release centers were an invaluable stepping-stone on the road back.

J. Edgar Hoover's inflexible attitude remained a seri-ous problem in spite of the demonstrable results of the parole program. As one of my colleagues within the

Department of Justice, he had ample opportunity to vent an aggressive opposition to what he termed my soft-on-crime policy. A newcomer to this august body of some 30 powerful division heads, I was tempted to respond with restraint at department meetings, or even worse, not at all. I would let the record speak for itself.

Things came to a crisis in August, 1958, when Hoover addressed the American Bar Association's annual convention at the Statler Hotel in Los Angeles. After a very hard-hitting address, he turned his big guns on probation and the parole system with a vengeance. His speech was carried by every major paper across the nation. A crime-weary public loved it. Hoover had again confirmed himself as the people's watchdog.

The Washington press pack pursued me. What did I have to say about the charges? Was there accord within the Justice Department? A running feud between our two divisions? A personality clash between Hoover and myself? I promised the press that I would clarify the issues the following month in a speech I was scheduled to make in the same hotel before the National Exchange Club's annual convention.

At long last I had the opportunity of publicly taking on the giant among America's public servants. Hours went into the preparation of my rebuttal to Mr. Hoover's specific and general charges against parole. Three days before my slated appearance, I sent a copy to the then Attorney General, Bill Rogers. In very short order he phoned his reaction. "George, that speech will hit the headlines and will put me right in the middle between two divisions of the Department of Justice."

"But, Bill, those things need to be said. They're long overdue," I bristled.

"Okay, George, suppose you take out these three paragraphs (he indicated three references which he felt were counterproductive in tone and content) and you'll have an excellent, defensible appeal that will insure press and public support. That's what you want, isn't it?"

Indeed, it *was* what I wanted, and I acquiesced.

Winging my way in to Los Angeles the next night, I was again captivated by the dazzling display of lights that illumined this sprawling megalopolis. The glitter seemed appropriate, a fitting way to showcase the wealth, the glamour, the showbiz dazzle that the City of the Queen of the Angels breathed. And yet, those lights could not blind me to the fact that in 1958 Los Angeles already had a serious crime problem. It was an appropriate place to state my case in clear and unmistakable terms. Down there, nestled against the foothills of the San Gabriel mountains, was Pasadena, where the dream had begun. Now those dreams had moved into the arena of real life, and I must let neither the seductive chimera of this western Camelot nor the loud and insistent voice of a detractor deter me.

That night I prayed: for the news conference at nine o'clock next morning; for the speech itself, scheduled for one hour later; for grace, poise, and ability to answer in a courageous yet Christian spirit my powerful adversary. If I were indeed implementing God's plans in this most important area of national concern, then their success was His responsibility. "God is the Judge . . . God is the Judge . . . God is the Judge . . . God is . . . ." Psalm 75:6,7 became a soothing litany of reassurance as I sank into sleep.

At nine o'clock the next morning, I walked into the news conference room to the glare of flashbulbs and TV lights. In an opening statement, I took note of Mr. Hoover's tough speech the month before, but reminded reporters that the FBI and the U.S. Parole Board were independent divisions within the Department and that, although my pending speech would defend parole, it was the Attorney General's policy that differences between division heads be debated and settled within their closed weekly meetings.

For the next 45 minutes I fielded the media's questions but doggedly refused to attack Mr. Hoover. When the news conference was over, 50 members of the news teams, including TV cameramen from the three major networks with their equipment, followed me into the packed ballroom of the Statler Hotel.

The introduction was brief, laudatory, upbeat. Quickly and confidently I approached the podium, acknowledged the applause, and began.

In this day when the total resources of the Western World have been committed to the defense of freedom itself, it is well for us in America to take stock not only of our military strength but to re-evaluate our total resources. This includes a new look at not only our supply of steel, oil, wheat or atomic bombs, but a look at our human resources as well. If we are to emerge final victors over the power of the Kremlin, it will require that we make full use not only of our "front line fighting men," but that we shall make every effort to salvage some of the less capable and less desirable raw material as well. *

That evening all three television networks and newspapers across the nation gave very complete and

---

* For an edited text of the complete speech see Appendix B.

favorable coverage to my speech. Of even greater significance to me was the meeting I had, at his request, with Mr. Hoover a few weeks later. He had initiated the contact; he wanted to discuss some matters pertaining to an inmate of Terre Haute Federal Prison.

On the designated day, Hoover and a bodyguard arrived at my office. "Mr. Chairman, I have a problem with the case," he began and proceeded to elaborate for about 20 minutes.

When he had finished, I said, "Mr. Hoover, I also have a problem and need your help."

A bit startled, Hoover responded, "Please, let me know how I can help."

"I must tell you, Mr. Hoover, that our department has been hurt—badly hurt—by your criticism. The public's image of the parole system has been damaged. We need to talk about that."

Hoover admitted readily that, yes, the Attorney General had talked to him about this problem. "But, George," he insisted, "when I've questioned parole, I've really been referring to the state level. They're being entirely too permissive. Not the federal sector, George. Not that."

I had no trouble agreeing with Hoover on his assessment of the state parole system, which at that time badly needed to modernize and strengthen its programs. At the same time, I felt sure that in the future Mr. Hoover would judiciously draw a distinction between state and federal parole policies in public and private utterances.

A few weeks later I received an invitation to have lunch in his private dining room with Director Hoover and three of his top assistants. The atmosphere was pleasant, even affable, and afterward we posed for pictures in his private office. From that time on, until his death in 1972, we enjoyed a warm and intimate friendship. It was a reconciliation that lent an added dimension to the respect I felt for him as a professional.

Little did I suspect, when I attended this great man's funeral on May 2, 1972, that the man seated just three rows ahead of me, at that time Deputy Attorney General Patrick Gray III, would be designated as Hoover's successor. Neither could I have imagined the fury that would one day be unleashed by the far left against the top command of the FBI, seated in bowed sorrow before me. The man we mourned had forged, in the course of a long and distinguished career, the best intelligence and law-enforcement agency in the world. Yet, against the FBI and the CIA would be mounted a very successful campaign to destroy their effectiveness. As intended, the nation's internal security would be dangerously weakened and its intelligence-gathering capability severely diminished.

Despite Hoover's critics, history will, in retrospect, award him high points in putting the welfare of the Republic above all personal and lesser considerations in exercising his considerable power and authority during a period of grave danger to our national security.

11
Treason in High Places

Two men went up into the temple to
pray....[One] stood and prayed thus with
himself: God, I thank thee that I am not as other
men are, extortioners, unjust.... The [other]
...smote upon his breast, saying, God be mer-
ciful to me a sinner.

The walls of Lewisburg Federal Maximum Security
Prison at Lewisburg, Pennsylvania, rose an awesome 22
feet high into the late summer sky. As by successive stages
I entered that enormous complex, I wondered how a
newly arrived prisoner must feel when confronted with
its vast machinery of incarceration. To get *in* was a major
operation; to get *out*—before one's time—was an impossible dream.

Amazingly, there had been an escape just three years
before. One of the prisoners had taken a doctor hostage,
knife at this throat. He had gotten through one gate after
another and out to the control gate, where a guard raised

his gun. "If you shoot, I'll slit his throat," snarled the convict and pressed the knife into the soft flesh of the terrified doctor's neck. The guard lowered his weapon. The would-be escapee tasted an hour or so of freedom before capture. Except for that one brief and ill-fated flight, Lewisburg deserved its designation as a "maximum security" prison.

I was there that last week in August 1953, as part of an orientation program to acquaint me with the federal parole process. Under the tutelage of Dr. George Killenger, fellow member of the Parole Board and its former chairman under President Truman, I toured the facility and watched as he conducted parole violation and parole hearings for those eligible from among the 2000 or so federal prisoners housed within Lewisburg's walls.

The next day Dr. Killenger and I were in deep conversation as we walked with the warden from the hearing room to the officers' dining hall. "You'll want to see where the inmates eat," Dr. Killenger interrupted, pausing at an open doorway. As we entered together, he explained that the huge and elaborate room had been one of the more fanciful WPA projects of the thirties. It even boasted a number of statues, whose creators were no doubt aspiring or down-on-their-luck artists who perhaps otherwise would never have found a showcase for their work.

A long line of men in single formation shuffled slowly toward the steam tables on the far side of the dining room, their prison garb contrasting strangely with the ornate decor of their surroundings. When finished, they would desposit their dishes and utensils in the designated bins and pause at the exit for a metal detector check. Blunt and dull-edged knives and even spoons were coveted "souvenirs" and had been known to turn up later ingeniously refashioned as lethal weapons.

"There, that's Alger Hiss!" Dr. Killenger nudged me and pointed to one of the slowly moving figures in the line. I found myself studying Lewisburg's most renowned inmate. Convicted of perjury, suspected of espionage, the man I saw before me bore an unmistakable refinement of face and figure. Evidencing neither boisterous camaraderie nor sullen wariness, nor indeed any identifiable emotion in between, Hiss seemed a man apart. As I was to learn later, he had come to terms with prison life. Asking for no privileges, he invited no confidences and encouraged no friendships. Dr. Killenger described Hiss as "highly intelligent but most noncommunicative" during his first unsuccessful parole hearing on November 24, 1952. At his next application I would need to be ready to pass judgment.

Upon returning to Washington, I pulled the Hiss file for a thoroughgoing study. I felt a heavy responsibility. Here was a high-ranking state department official who had been convicted of perjury. The record showed that Hiss had been the target of investigation by the FBI for more than six years. During all that time the Bureau had failed to come up with the evidence it needed to make a case. It was the persistent efforts of Richard Nixon and the House Unamerican Activities Committee that had finally brought the case to a head, forcing a grand jury confrontation at which Hiss had perjured himself. The statute of limitations had run out, precluding conviction for alleged espionage activities during the 1930's.

For the record, however, the government had accused Hiss of turning over many sensitive documents to the Soviets, documents dealing with major issues then dominating world affairs: the Sino-Japanese War, the German takeover of Austria, the Spanish Civil War, suspected German designs on Czechoslovakia, Japanese threats to interests in Asia, and the attitude of major

European and Asian powers toward the Soviet Union. In short, there was scarcely an important area of world affairs which Hiss's alleged activities had not breached.

The list of ingredients in what was to become one of our nation's most bizarre and frustrating espionage trials was itself bizarre: an elusive Woodstock typewriter, a secondhand Ford of questionable disposition, a rare species of migratory bird, a *pumpkin* containing a cache of government documents, and a conscience-stricken former member of the Communist Party.

The two principals in the case, Alger Hiss and Whittaker Chambers, couldn't have had more disparate backgrounds and personalities. Son of a Baltimore, Maryland, dry goods salesman father and a teacher mother, Alger had been named for that prototype American hero, Horatio Alger. Like him, he early learned the work ethic. Four mornings a week, he and a friend arose at 5:30 to deliver springwater to the houses in the surrounding German community. His was a religious home. Church was a must and was augmented by daily Bible reading. Prep school was followed by scholarships, first to Johns Hopkins University and then to Harvard Law School. Recognized as a bright young man with a brilliant future, he was appointed upon graduation as law clerk to Supreme Court Justice Oliver Wendell Holmes, one of our nation's all-time greats in the judicial system.

From there Hiss moved rapidly up through the ranks. Time spent in a prestigious law firm was a springboard to the Justice Department and finally to the State Department. By World War II Hiss had become, as the Hearst Press was to claim in court, "a confidant of President Roosevelt." He was present in 1944 at the Dumbarton Oaks Economic Conference as Secretary to the American delegation. At Yalta, where so much of Europe was handed over to Stalin, Hiss was at President Roosevelt's side. As Secretary General of the San Francisco conference at which the United Nations was born, he was to a large extent the architect of its charter. His accomplishments during and after the war years were crowned in 1947, when at 43 years of age Alger Hiss became the President of the Carnegie Endowment for International Peace. It seemed a fitting capstone to a meteoric career.

Perhaps the life of Whittaker Chambers was, in part, an even truer prototype of the Horatio Alger story. In stark contrast to the rectitude and propriety which marked Alger Hiss's family life, Whittaker's was a shambles of broken relationships: a father who deserted his family, a neurotic mother who slept with an axe under her pillow, a suicidal brother, and a bullying drunkard of a grandfather. Not surprisingly, Whittaker ran away from home after completing high school and adopted a series of assumed names for a time. His life hardly had the ingredients of a success story. Yet from this unlikely past, Whittaker Chambers would eventually rise to become a senior editor of *Time* magazine.

Few would have suspected such ultimate success from Chambers's less-than-distinguished university career. After two years at Columbia, he dropped out to join the Communist Party. His stay at the university had been marked by brief forays into writing—a blasphemous play about Christianity, which he termed "a sadistic religion," and a smattering of pornographic verse. His conviction that his world was dying and that Communism was "history's surgeon" to "save the wreckage of man" had developed slowly in those years since childhood. Perhaps his own failure as a human being within society was the prime mover in his fateful decision to become involved in espionage. That career was aborted also with his abandonment of the Communist cause. "Two faiths are on trial," Chambers wrote in the preface to *Witness*, his impassioned apologia for his painful descent and ultimate resurrection. He began that book with the lines:

> In 1937, I began, like Lazarus, the impossible return. I began to break away from communism and to climb from deep within its underground, where for six years I had been buried, back into the world of free men. "When we dead awaken. . ." I used sometimes to say to my wife, who, though never a communist, had shared my revolutionary hopes and was now to share my ordeals. "When we dead awaken. . . ." I felt a surging release and a sense of freedom, like a man who bursts at last gasp out of a drowning sea.*

Conscience demanded a further step, he was to claim—to come clean about his past to the government he had sinned against. Inevitably, confession would implicate his onetime friend Alger Hiss. The denouement came about, however, in a most unlikely way.

The Hiss-Chambers connection came to public attention by virtue of Chambers's one talent, and it was a considerable one—writing. In 1938, a year after his final defection from the Communist Party, he was contacted for an interview on his former activities in the underground by rabid anticommunist Herbert Solow. Herbert seemed just the man to evaluate a manuscript that Chambers had prepared on the subject. Although it was never published, the manuscript's contents soon became known. Solow was not one to allow fresh ammunition for his obsession to lie about unused.

---

* (Random House, 1952)

The manuscript soon came to the attention of ultra-conservative journalist Issac Levine, who quickly saw a newsworthy story and urged Chambers to allow him to arrange an interview with Assistant Secretary of State Adolf Berle. At this fateful juncture, Alger Hiss's name first came to government attention as a potential security risk. He was one of 18 persons who, Chambers claimed, had been known to him as members of the Communist underground.

In the meantime, the FBI had been independently investigating Chamber's Communist past, and in 1942 its agents questioned him—without, however, eliciting anything new. But they felt they were definitely onto something in November 1945, when Hiss was accused of wartime espionage activities by Communist courier Elizabeth Bentley, the "Red Spy Queen," as the tabloids had labeled her. The FBI ordered a wiretap on the Hiss home. It proceeded to alert the appropriate government agencies by a series of memoranda. Its Chief, J. Edgar Hoover, attempted to orchestrate Hiss's "resignation." Finally Hiss was summoned by the FBI for an interview. It was all to no avail. Hiss denied all allegations, and there was no hard evidence to prove otherwise.

The years 1945-48 were frustrating ones for the conservative right, which was attempting to expose and to authenticate what it deemed to be the grave threat of Communist subversion. There seemed ample reason for alarm. Charges flew—in the press, on the floor of Congress, in memos from the FBI, in testimony from former Communists, from Soviet defectors. And the public, as a whole, believed what they heard.

On August 3, 1948, the suspicions, the allegations, the nebulous uncertainties all seemed to merge and take tangible shape in the public mind as Whittaker Chambers

stood before the House Unamerican Activities Committee
and testified:

> I served the communist underground. . . . I
> knew at its top level a group of seven or so men.
> One member of the group was Alger Hiss. . . .
> The original purpose of the apparatus was
> the communist infiltration of the American
> government.

Chambers went on to describe Hiss as a "dedicated and
disciplined communist" from whom he collected party
dues for approximately three years. He further alleged
that on at least 50 occasions during 1937-38, Hiss had
taken classified State Department documents home,
where either he or his wife Priscilla had typed them on
their Woodstock typewriter. From there the papers had
gone by Chambers's hand to Colonel Bykov, head of a
Soviet underground spy ring.

The stunning realization that a man who even now
stood so close to the nerve center of American—Soviet
relations could be a Communist agent was overlaid by
a moment of pathos when Chambers painted the scene
of their last meeting. He claimed that after his own change
of heart, he made one final visit to the Hiss home in
Washington D.C. to try to talk Alger into breaking with
the Party. They had argued all night, but Hiss, with tears
streaming down his face, had refused to renounce his trea-
sonous allegiance.

In recounting the break with his former friend, Chambers declared before the committee:

> I do not hate Mr. Hiss. We were caught in
> a tragedy of history. I testified against him with
> remorse and pity, but in the moment of history

in which this nation now stands, so help me God, I could not do otherwise.

Alger Hiss responded to Chambers's testimony with a telegram to the HUAC requesting an opportunity for rebuttal, a request which was promptly granted. In the days to follow Hiss would make a fateful appearance before Richard Nixon, junior member of the HUAC and doggedly determined to pursue what seemed at best a blatant cover-up and at worst the tip of an espionage iceberg.

In testimony, Hiss categorically denied that he had ever been a member of the Communist party or had known Whittaker Chambers. With that sworn declaration, things seemed to be at an impasse.

When HUAC debated the advisability of abandoning the inquiry, Nixon took up the ball. He requested full responsibility for heading up a subcommittee to concentrate on whether the two principals had indeed been acquainted in the thirties. And thus he at least had the ingredients for a perjury trial—someone was not telling the truth.

The inquiry now took on a newly energized character. Chambers proceeded to astonish the Committee and indeed the nation with a seeming wealth of personal knowledge of Hiss. Of particular interest was his claim that he had for a time lived rent-free in Hiss's apartment and had been given the use of an old Ford as part of the deal as well.

For his part, Hiss denied ever having seen Chambers. He acknowledged, however, that he had in fact sublet his apartment to a man he had known for perhaps six months, a free-lance writer named George Crosley. Then, at a surprise confrontation between the two men arranged by HUAC, Hiss had at first registered confusion when asked to identify the man before him. "Would the man please say a few words?" Hiss requested. It seemed that Hiss did know him after all. He identified Chambers as "George Crosley."

Nothing that had been uncovered so far offered any concrete proof of wrongdoing on Hiss's part. Clearly they were not both telling the truth; something was needed to crack the wall of deceit. At this point Chambers accepted an invitation to appear on "Meet The Press." Hiss had goaded him to repeat his accusations outside the hearing room, where he would then be subject to a suit for libel. Chambers was only too happy to oblige via radio.

Had Hiss only been bluffing? Apparently not. He promptly filed a 50,000-dollar libel suit against his accuser. That proved to be a fatal mistake. Hiss had little to fear from HUAC, because the statute of limitations had run out on any possible charge of espionage. False testimony in court, however, was perjury—and that was the charge taken up by a Federal Grand Jury.

That powerful judicial body limited itself to two questions: Had Alger Hiss ever turned over any classified government documents to Whittaker Chambers; and had Hiss, contrary to his solemn denials, ever seen Chambers after January 1, 1937? The documents possessed by Chambers all bore a later date. The unequivocal response by Hiss to both questions was "No."

As part of the court exhibits, Chambers submitted 65 typewritten pages of secret State Department documents and several handwritten notes, all bearing dates between January 5 and April 1, 1938. Two weeks later, Chambers reported to Nixon that he had additional documents at his Westminster, Maryland, farm. With 24 hours HUAC investigators converged on the farm and followed

Chambers to a pumpkin patch, where he proceeded to remove from a very ordinary-looking pumpkin more than 50 frames of microfilmed documents bearing the date January 14, 1938. The disclosures seemed to furnish all the evidence the Grand Jury needed, and an indictment was accordingly drawn up and a trial date set for May 31, 1949.

The trial of Alger Hiss began in an emotionally charged atmosphere. Chambers admitted readily enough that he had perjured himself both before the House Unamerican Activities Committee and the Grand Jury, particularly in the matter of contradictory testimony relevant to espionage charges against Hiss.

Mrs. Chambers, however, became fair game for a withering cross-examination by Defense Attorney Lloyd Stryker after her detailed and intimate revelations of the relationship which had existed between the two families in the thirties. It was the type of day-to-day minutia that a woman would tend to remember but could also easily be broken down under the pressures of the witness box. Insistently, Mrs. Chambers stuck to her recollected trivia and responded with angry tears when Stryker flung insulting remarks at her about her husband's character and testimony.

The trial soon focused on the Woodstock typewriter. The defense did not deny that the written documents were in Hiss's hand. Neither did it deny that the Woodstock had belonged to the Hiss family. But did the typewritten pages originate in the machine in question? To arrive at that answer, government witness and FBI typewriter expert Amos Freeman took the stand. He declared that upon comparison of the government material with other documents admittedly typed on the Woodstock, he could definitely certify them to be from the same machine.

The defense had an answer. It put Clytie Catlett on the witness stand. She had been a maid, she testified, in the Hiss's home during the period in question. She readily claimed to remember that her sons had been given an old typewriter when the Hisses had moved to their Georgetown home in 1937. The documents under scrutiny were all dated in early 1938. Mrs. Catlett's son Mike took a look at the typewriter, pecked a few keys, and declared it was the machine that he and his brother had been given more than ten years before.

Seventeen days into the trial, Hiss entered the witness stand. He made a good initial impression as he guardedly responded to questions from defense counsel. Under cross-examination, however, from prosecuting attorney Thomas Murphy, the fact was established that in the early thirties Hiss had been a member of the International Juridical Association, cited by HUAC as a Communist front organization. Nothing further was uncovered.

Attention returned to the typewriter when Priscilla Hiss was cross-examined. Whereas she had claimed before the Grand Jury that she did not type, she now testified that she was a proficient typist. Her calm veneer was further cracked when she was shown photostatic proof of her 1932 registration in the Socialist Party. She had denied ever being a member.

At the conclusion of the five-week trial, prosecutor Murphy faced the jury with confidence: "The documents in evidence are as damning as a child coming out of the pantry, mouth smeared with raspberry preserves." He again outlined the facts upon which he expected the jury to declare Hiss guilty: that documents dated 1938 and accessible only to Hiss were in the possession of his friend Whittaker Chambers, and that the documents were either in Hiss's handwriting or typed on his typewriter.

The jury was not entirely convinced. It was hung at

eight guilty and four not guilty. The case would be tried again.

For a further nine weeks, from November 17 until January 21, both sides went over the same ground—and more. This time the jury would hear Chambers described by a psychiatrist as a psychopath, a liar, a sick personality who had effected assumed names in order to live out his neurotic fantasies. Murphy ripped into his testimony. Psychiatry purported to give definitive answers which under scrutiny proved to be as nebulous as the theories upon which they were based. The jury was treated to a state of the arts sparring match between two immovable protagonists.

The most damaging witness on behalf of the prosecution was Edith Murray, who had worked as a maid for the Chambers family in 1935-36. She testified that they had upon several occasions received a visitor who "lived in Washington" and who was addressed as "Miss Priscilla." On one occasion she had been accompanied by her husband. Mrs. Murray pointed to Alger and Priscilla Hiss. "They were the visitors," she declared.

When it was all over, the 110 witnesses, the 423 exhibits, and the more than one million words of testimony convinced the jury. In just less than 24 hours they came up with a guilty verdict on two counts of perjury. Judge Goddard imposed two sentences of five years, to run concurrently, one for each count.

As Hiss stood before Judge Goddard for sentencing, he referred again to the damning evidence of the Woodstock typewriter. "I am confident," he said, "that in the future, the full facts of how Whittaker Chambers was able to carry out forgery by typewriter will be disclosed." Such facts, if they exist, have never been brought to light.

The Supreme Court refused to review the case, and an appeal failed. On March 22, 1951, Hiss was shackled and transported to Lewisburg Federal Penitentiary.

As it was in the Rosenberg case, the Hiss trial continued to be fought by the media and in the public mind outside the courtroom. Secretary of State Dean Acheson vowed he would not turn his back on a trusted friend. Eleanor Roosevelt, avid supporter of liberal causes, found it "rather horrible" that the jury had chosen to believe Chambers rather than Hiss. There were cries of "victim" and "hysteria" and "red herring." Still, most people believed the evidence and accepted the verdict as just.

It was a long step down from honored State Department official to prison warehouse clerk. Lewisburg records described Alger Hiss as "not particularly happy, yet he managed the difficult task of maintaining his dignity and composure." Perhaps things went better for him than might otherwise have been expected in such a hostile environment, because he cultivated the association of the prison's Mafia element, whom he perceived as "prisoners of war." He openly expressed admiration for the close-knit, protective, family relationship exhibited by these imprisoned mobsters. A prominent Communist inmate, also named by Elizabeth Bentley in FBI hearings, was murdered by a fellow prisoner. For a physically nonaggressive intellectual like Hiss, it was important to have some kind of inside protection within the intricate and shadowy hierarchy of power and payoffs that exist even within prison walls.

One year after Hiss's first parole appeal was turned down, he was allowed to petition for reconsideration. The Federal Parole Board hearing room was packed with sympathizers and supporters. Leading the plea for parole was Paul Robeson, noted opera singer, who was to eventually make a ringing denunciation of the United States and move to Russia.

The emotion generated by Alger Hiss's well-wishers

had no effect upon the Board. We denied his application for parole for the second time. Based on the record, my own vote reflected my conviction, then and now, that Hiss was guilty of far more than perjury.

Hiss was destined to complete his full term at Lewisburg Prison, less good-time credits. After 44 months behind bars, he was released on November 27, 1954.

During the years since then, I have heard hundreds of security cases under the jurisdiction of the United States Board of Parole. I find myself agreeing with Hiss's prosecutor, Thomas Murphy. His final appeal to the jury in the second trial bears repeating:

> . . . take them with you to the jury room, those photographs; take the instruments. What do they prove? Ladies and gentlemen, it proves treason, and *that* is the traitor.

12
Fear No President

Promotion cometh neither from the east nor
from the west nor from the south. But God is
the Judge: He putteth down one and setteth up
another.

My appointment with President Eisenhower in the Oval
Office of the White House that May morning of 1953 had
ushered in what was to be a happy and productive
12-year tenure with the United States Board of Parole.
The assassin's bullet that struck down John Fitzgerald
Kennedy and which brought to power his Vice President,
Lyndon Johnson, was to be my undoing. The chain of
events had the aura of inevitability.

The giant of a man who was Dwight D. Eisenhower had
infused the nation with faith and confidence through his
leadership. There was a sense of security, a visible heal-
ing of the nation's war wounds, a profound conviction
that a fundamental righteousness prevailed in the halls
of government and in the fabric of society. Americans

were unabashedly patriotic and wore their "I like Ike" buttons with genuine pride. Eisenhower was Abeline's all-American boy, West Point's five star general, Mamie's boyfriend, young David's grandfather, and the President of all the people. He listened to the voices of America, and he listened to me when my program was in trouble and I needed help.

President Eisenhower showed his confidence in my leadership by appointing me to two consecutive six-year terms. I had just begun my second term when Kennedy, the young representative from Massachusettes, narrowly defeated Vice President Richard Nixon in the 1960 election. Teamed with Lyndon Johnson, young Kennedy voiced inspiring hopes for a "New Frontier," in which the public good would replace individual interests. Americans across the land caught at the magic of the words from his inaugural speech: "Ask not what your country can do for you; ask what you can do for your country."

It soon became apparent that Camelot-on-the-Potomac was to introduce a new image of youth and vigor. A few days after his inauguration, the new President announced the appointment of his younger brother Robert Kennedy as Attorney General. The press reaction—and mine—was one of surprise. "Bobby," with little legal experience behind him, was to become head of the Justice Department, the nation's biggest law office?

The transformation continued. An army of young lawyers descended on the prestigious and very formal "Palace of Justice," wearing Ivy League suits, effecting glasses pushed up on shocks of wayward hair, and speaking with a decidedly Bostonian accent.

As was routine, I, along with all presidential appointees, tendered my resignation as Chairman of the United States Board of Parole. Six weeks later the entire Board received a summons to appear before the new Attorney General.

There was considerable grumbling, especially from the older members, when I announced the meeting scheduled for the following week. Who was this novice who had been catapulted to such high office? That was a question frequently and pointedly asked. Keeping my real thoughts to myself, I reminded all the members that, although the U.S. Parole Board was an independent federal agency, we were nevertheless by statute placed within the Justice Department and were required to report to the President through the Attorney General on administrative and budget matters.

What I knew, but the Board members did not, was that Bobby Kennedy had already looked into the legal possibilities of replacing all Republician appointees on the Parole Board. I knew, of course, that such a partisan move was impossible. Board appointees could be removed only for sufficient cause, including an act of moral turpitude. Nevertheless, I was more than a little apprehensive as I and my fellow members entered the Attorney General's regal conference room.

After introductions, I heard myself assuring the Attorney General of the assembled Board members' loyalty and their willingness to serve in whatever capacity he and the President should desire.

Uncomfortably, Kennedy removed his feet from the desk, readjusted his loosened tie, and pulled his glasses into place. Then he proceeded with what he really had on his mind. "When will your term of office be up?" he asked each man in turn.

When he got to our two senior members, each stated the facts requested and added coldly that they expected to serve every day of their unfinished terms, but not one day longer.

I hastily thanked the Attorney General, motioned to my colleagues, and ushered them out the door as quickly as possible.

Robert Kennedy lent some grace to an awkward situation when, a few days later, he requested my opinion as to who should chair the Board. I strongly recommended my longtime and well-qualified friend, Richard Chappell, a Georgia Democrat. Kennedy requested that I stay on as vice chairman. I acquiesced, and by executive order of the new President, Chairman Chappell and I launched out on the necessary reorganization of the Parole Board under the new administration.

The two of us worked well together and were looking forward to a productive tenure. Although the young Kennedy brothers did not show the same personal interest in the work of the Justice Department and the Parole Board as Eisenhower and Brownell had, I felt we had a working relationship.

Camelot's hopes and dreams were shattered on November 22, 1963, by the sharp crack of rifle fire. Our dynamic young President, his life fast ebbing away, slumped helplessly in his wife's arms as the world watched in horror. Aboard Air Force One, within minutes of Kennedy's death, Lyndon Baines Johnson was sworn in as the thirty-sixth President of the United States.

We had often met before. As chairman of the Senate Finance Committee, Johnson had proven to be a tough inquisitor when I presented our yearly budget for approval. I well remembered the budget hearings of June of 1959. It was obvious that things would be sticky when Chairman Johnson had begun by jumping all over Attorney General William Rogers on his presentation of the Justice Department budget. When my turn had come, Johnson had grilled me on every new item requested. Then he had broadened his attacks to a general charge that our department was too tough and hadn't paroled enough federal prisoners. I had fielded questions about parole policies, but had gotten the decided idea that the Chairman had a major problem with my philosophy.

In November 1963, when Johnson became "President by assassination," I realized I would need help if I were to be reappointed when my term of office expired in January of 1965. Vice President Humphrey and Senate Minority Leader Everett Dirksen, among others, appealed to Johnson directly and reported back that the President had assured them I was slated for a third six-year term. Somehow I didn't count on it.

Five months later, while conducting routine parole hearings at Terre Haute Federal Prison in Indiana, I faced, unknown to me, a labor racketeer who was to be my undoing. The applicant had been involved in business dealings with the mob, and as his case unfolded, I became convinced that his release was not in the public interest. The panel of three judges came up with a majority vote denying parole.

An ominous undercurrent of rumblings began immediately upon my return to Washington. The White House wanted this particular prisoner paroled *immediately*. Didn't I know he had headed up a union fund-raising drive for President Johnson's reelection campaign? Didn't I realize that my present term expired in eight months? Wasn't it obvious to me, as it was to everyone else, that I was committing political suicide?

Calmly I assured the powers that be that I would refer the case before the entire eight-member board for reappraisal. Despite the best that the applicant's two very capable lawyers could do, when the hearing was completed the full board turned in a six-to-two vote sustaining my original order denying parole.

"I'm sorry . . . the President has changed his mind about

your reappointment," Vice President Humphrey informed me apologetically a few days later. "I'll keep working on it. I'm terribly sorry," he repeated. It was I who felt sorry for him. The news he had brought had hardly come as a surprise.

On a cold April morning in 1965, three months after my term of office had expired, I was on the Pennsylvania Turnpike heading west. Behind me were 12 years of devoted service in a subcabinet level of the Federal government. Gone were the power and the prestige. Behind me were my lovely Maryland home and wife. Lois had stayed on while I went in search of a new job.

Somewhere on that turnpike not too far from home, the enormity of it all overwhelmed me and I burst into tears. Hadn't I served God faithfully and truly during those 12 years? Hadn't I kept covenant with Him, daring to "fear no man," not even my President? Doubts now came in a flood. Perhaps I had been a little *too* zealous in that vow. Perhaps I had needlessly sacrificed my family's security, my son's future.

The pain and the doubts raged for nearly two hours as I in turn fought, succumbed to, and rationalized with the tempter seated beside me in the car. He stirred my cup of bitterness as he reminded me that surely a proper humility demanded a less adamant stand on critical questions of judgment. He reminded me that the completion of another six-year term would have qualified me for a well-paid retirement for the rest of my life.

Drained at last by sheer weariness and a surfeit of emotion, I seemed to awaken slowly to a sense of calm. The storm had spent itself. Unbidden, a verse from Nehemiah 8 came to mind: "The joy of the Lord is your strength," the prophet had declared. Had I been so ungrateful as to forget all of God's bounty to me during the past 12 years? And couldn't I trust Him to show the same care in the future? With a sense of exhilaration and authority, I commanded Satan, the wily tempter of the past two hours, to leave me. And he did. It was a practical lesson I needed from God's hands. Christian though I was, I needed to experience the reality of Satan's wiles and the reality of victory in Jesus Christ. The rest of the day He Himself was present with me as I filled the car with songs and prayers of praise and thanksgiving.

After spending a few days of spring vacation with my college son, George Calvert, in Idaho, I headed on to Nevada to talk with Richard Campbell, Chairman of the Nevada State Board of Probation and Parole Services. He and his board had considered 61 applicants for the position of Chief of Probation and Parole for the State of Nevada. I was their unanimous choice.

A further interview with Governor Grant Sawyer in his Carson City office that afternoon indicated that I had passed scrutiny there as well. He informed me that on that very morning the State Senate had passed a new modified-indeterminate-sentencing law over Republican objections. I reminded him that I was a conservative Republican but I had always run a bipartisan, nonpolitical correctional program. I wanted no politicking or infighting to impede my work. I also laid on the table the problems that had cost me my job in Washington.

The Governor, a Democrat, dismissed the thought of any problems in Nevada. Probations and parole would be kept strictly above politics, he assured me. When he further announced that the legislature had just agreed to substantially raise the salary of the new Parole and Probation Chief, the job looked almost too good. A quick call to Lois assured me that she agreed to the move, and I informed the Governor that I would accept the appointment. Thus, a bare ten days since I had left Washington in abject despair, and within 24 hours of my arrival in the Nevada State Capital, I found myself again employed.

The new legislation on indeterminate sentencing, erroneously dubbed an "early parole" law by its detractors, was thrown at me at my first press conference— the very day after my appointment, which was also the day after my arrival in Carson City.

"How do you plan to administer the new law?" reporters demanded as they swarmed all over me. I explained that the new statute merely clarified an old, outdated one that had permitted past parole boards to release state prison felons before they had served their maximum terms. It also gave greater flexibility to the parole board's decision-making capabilities.

The press's interest was indeed apropos. The leading critic of the new legislation was the District Attorney, William Raggio, a Republican who very much wanted Governor Sawyer's job. It was he and a fellow Republican, Lieutenant Governor Paul Laxalt, who had tagged the new legislation an "early parole" law. The two men joined forces to criticize me, a Republican, for taking an appointment under a Democratically controlled administration. "Soft on crime" was one of the congenital sins of the Democrats, and I was guilty by association.

As I flew around the state, meeting key legislators, law enforcement officials, and members of the news media, I discovered that the new parole law had developed into a very hot issue. Democrats and Republicans were clearly divided. I concluded that my first task was to gain the confidence of the public by assuring them that my program of criminal justice would benefit *all* the people of Nevada, both inside and outside prison walls.

From the news media I had, in general, little to fear. Most followed the lead of Hank Greenspan, owner and editor of the powerful *Las Vegas Sun*, who assured me of his newspaper's full support if I would "call them" as fairly in Nevada as I had in Washington.

Some papers were cautious. The *Reno Evening Gazette* did not overstate the situation when it titled a lead article "Parole Chief Reed Faces Tough Job in Nevada." It correctly pinpointed the real question: Which side would get the greatest political mileage out of the new indeterminate parole law—the Republicans or the Democrats?

Approval or no, I launched a five-pronged program to help change Nevada's dubious distinction of having the highest crime rate in the country. I began with a complete reorganization of the parole department. A part of that revamping was the establishment of two new regional offices in Reno and Elko. Then a statewide commission was set up with a view to coordinating all correctional services under a new Nevada Department of Corrections. Of major significance was the revision of Nevada's Criminal Code, which hadn't been updated for nearly a hundred years. Finally, a new medium-security prison was opened just south of the capital, thus relieving the overcrowding at the old territorial maximum security prison east of the city. This expansion made possible the establishment of a classification and treatment program at both institutions.

My first annual report, for 1965, indicated that I had made good on my promise of the year before that my program would benefit *all* the people. Fewer paroles had been granted to felons—surely not an indication of a community-endangering policy. Of even more significance to me was the encouraging fact that there had been a 12 percent increase in the number of parolees making good.

On October 7, 1965, the very same day when I gave a speech outlining the year's progress before the Criminal Law Seminar, Lieutenant Governor Laxalt, now a Republican gubernatorial candidate, called for a repeal of the so-called "early parole" law. "It's given the impression that this state is soft on crime," he protested. "Here we are trying to give prisoners a break, and Nevada already has the highest crime rate in the country."

Unquestionably, his remarks hit a raw nerve among the electorate. With the pleasure palaces of Las Vegas and Reno so flamboyantly evident and with organized crime so unabashedly courting politicians, the voters were already too painfully aware of their state's reputation as a crime mecca. I responded vigorously, but despite my efforts to rescue my program from the political arena and to dispassionately outline and clarify our progress, Bill Raggio and Lieutenant Governor Laxalt continued to mount increasingly vitriolic attacks against me and Governor Sawyer.

Toward the end of my second year in Nevada, I found myself again in Washington, this time to represent the Governor at a meeting of the President's Crime Commission. News of my progress report on Nevada's new correctional program, in which I praised the people of Nevada for helping to make it a success, hit the headlines at home.

"Reed's statement in Washington to the President's Crime Commission is completely inaccurate." At the airport on my return, a dozen reporters asked me to comment on District Attorney Raggio's provocative claim to the press. The headlines had been explicit: "Raggio Disputes Reed's Report on Crime Praise." I held my fire at the airport. I wanted to read all the news releases and confer with Governor Sawyer before making a statement. At last I came to a decision: I would *not* let Raggio call me a liar.

The Sunday papers across the state headlined my response. "Reed Raps Raggio's Charges." My published statement accused the District Attorney of Washoe

County with deliberately trying to confuse the public for political purposes. Frankly, I was angry—and righteously so, I believed. The attempted destruction of a very promising corrections program was not a legitimate route to the top, in my opinion.

I followed my salvo with a quote from Robert Keldgard, Regional Director of the National Council on Crime and Delinquency, and author of the state's progress report for the recently held President's Crime Commission:

> Comparatively speaking, Nevada did very little in the first one hundred years of its history. Now, with the new program [and] under its new leadership, [it] should become a pacesetter and a leader in the field of corrections. . . .

I concluded with both barrels blazing: "I wish to inform Mr. Raggio that he is the first person in over 27 years of administering correctional programs at both the Federal and State levels who ever questioned my integrity."

When it was all over and the smoke had cleared, Paul Laxalt had been elected Governor. I proferred my resignation. It had been a hard-fought battle. I couldn't regret the energy expended or even the enemies made to try to save the innovative program. It had been a worthy cause, and it was tempting to let bitterness prevail. Defeat was an all-too-familiar memory.

Years later Paul Laxalt and I met again, this time in Washington D.C. I welcomed him there as Senator-elect from Nevada. We had a good laugh as we recalled the stormy days when we had battled each other so self-righteously in Carson City.

Later yet, while I was visiting Nevada, Bill Raggio, now Chairman of the Senate Judiciary Committee, welcomed me with great warmth and invited me to join him for the opening ceremonies of the State Senate. His introduction stunned me—pleasantly: "Members of the Senate and guests, may I present to you my good friend, Judge George Reed, one of the great reformers of the criminal justice system, both in Nevada and the nation's Capitol."

From the gusto and frontier flavor of Carson City to the rural peace of Visalia, California . . . to the overlay of academia in tree-shaded Eugene, Oregon—we experienced them all during our exile from the nation's capital. Our arrival in Visalia was not exactly happenstance. Many years before we had purchased a hundred-acre farm in Tulare County, California's vaunted "Garden of the Sun." By agreement, our good neighbor farmed the property. Thus I became a "gentleman farmer," hearing by mail or long-distance phone call (or on occasional trips west) about the progress of our grain and alfalfa and cotton. With our departure from Nevada we purchased a home in nearby Visalia, and I became a farmer in earnest. I celebrated by planting 20 acres in navel orange trees. The "Reed Ranch" was on its way.

Ranching was my hobby. Teaching was my passion. Hired as Professor of Criminology at College of the Sequoias, I was able to help bright young college students along toward their chosen field of criminal justice. Concurrently, I became more and more deeply involved in city and county government.

It was a good life. I was fully involved professionally. Lois and I were active in a fine, growing church. We both appreciated the even flow of small-town living. Still, I was restless. When my former boss and longtime friend Herman Stark took it upon himself to recommend me for appointment as director of the Lane County, Oregon, Juvenile Court Agency, my heart skipped a beat. In the midst of my busy farming routine mixed with academia

I had forgotten just how closely entwined with the whole fabric of the criminal justice system my heart and life were.

I hardly realized how I had missed it all until I stood up to be sworn in as Director of Lane County's juvenile court center, the most prestigious such facility in the nation. It had been the creation and labor of love of the Honorable William Fort, Chief Judge of the Circuit Court. It was an honor to join him and his highly qualified staff and to be back in the business of salvaging young lives.

Again life seemed good, satisfying, significant. Lois loved our newly built Southern colonial home. She had dreamed for years of transplanting a bit of the splendor of antebellum Virginia to her native Oregon. She was happy because I was happy. But God had one of those quick-change surprises up His sleeve.

We were eating breakfast on the rainy morning of March 30, 1969, when the phone rang and a crisp, businesslike voice informed me that Attorney General John Mitchell wanted to speak to me. Quickly I washed down the bacon and eggs with a half-cup of coffee. I hadn't been getting many calls from Washington lately.

When the Attorney General came on, he said that he and President Richard Nixon were offering me a reappointment as Chairman of the U.S. Parole Board for a new six-year term. I was stunned. I didn't trust myself to express my true feelings. I thanked him for his and the President's confidence in me, but begged a few days for consideration and also a chance to fly to Washington for further consultation. Reluctantly he agreed to the delay.

Bitter experience had taught me to "get it on paper." Accordingly, I typed up a ten-point statement of expectation. In view of my prior experience, some of those points will not be a surprise. They included: 1) the independence of the U.S. Parole Board in its decision-making powers; 2) a budget adequate to support needed professional staff; 3) Board salaries comparable to other major federal commissions; and 4) one million dollars to underwrite and implement a research project known as "Improved Parole Decision Making."

As I flew to Washington, the words of Psalm 75:6,7 were a well-remembered refrain: "For promotion cometh neither from the east, nor from the west, nor from the south. But God is the judge: He putteth down one and setteth up another." Those verses had guided me in the past, even though a conviction of their truth had been the means of my departure four years earlier. Now they were accompanying me back with a renewed sense of purpose.

I had left the capital crushed in spirit and wallowing in self-pity and defeat, doubting even the marching orders that God had given me when I first went to Washington. Now "Fear and serve God always, but fear no man" had been tested in the crucible of experience, and I could truly look back and say with the prophet Samuel, "Hitherto hath the Lord helped us" (1 Samuel 7:12). It had taken Moses 40 years on the far side of the desert to learn his lesson. Now I thanked God that He had seen fit to abbreviate our wilderness years to four, and prayed that I might be a wiser steward of His gifts as we returned to the nation's capital.

On May 6, 1969, in a moving ceremony in Attorney General John Mitchell's conference room, I was sworn in to the office I had vacated four years before. The very next week I addressed the United States Attorneys' Annual Conference in the capital. The news I had to share was grim. I pointed out that during the last four years under a liberal administration the Board had paroled over 20 percent more marginal or bad-parole risks than during the previous four years under the Eisenhower administration.

This 20.5 percent increase in parole failures concerned me greatly, and I made a public commitment that day to put in motion an immediate and drastic reversal of that trend for the public benefit. It was good to be back on the job. It was humbling to see how God had worked that miracle. And it was exhilarating to see how He had changed my song of mourning to one of praise.

13
Pied Piper of Death

Neither repented they of their murders, nor of their sorceries, nor of their fornication, nor of their thefts.

The year I returned to Washington, seven murders of such savagery occurred in Los Angeles that the case thereafter came to be identified by its principal perpetrator rather than by its most famous victim. Any understanding of its bizarre character, however, requires a long look back.

The man I faced in the small Terminal Island Prison hearing room in the first week of June 1956 was no ordinary prisoner. The file I had just received revealed that virtually nothing had ever gone right for this young man. He was living proof of Solomon's exhortation in reverse: "Train up a child in the way he should [not] go, and when he is old he will not depart from it."

Sixteen-year-old Kathleen Maddox couldn't remember whether it was November 11 or 12 of 1934 that her baby was born. His conception was casual; she was a Cincinnati prostitute. When little Charles interfered with business, she would leave him with the neighbors until his aunt and uncle would show up to claim him. In 1939 Kathleen was caught robbing a gas station and was sent to West Virginia State Penitentiary for five years. Again Charles went to his aunt. The three years that his mother served time were the most stable that Charles was ever to know.

When the young mother was released on parole, she reclaimed her eight-year-old son, and for the next five years "home" was a succession of sleazy hotel rooms and cheap apartments. The closest he ever came to knowing a father was the progression of men whom Kathleen passed off as "uncles."

Little Charles was increasingly an encumbrance. In 1947 Kathleen attempted to place him in a foster home. None was available. In desperation she put him in the Gibault School for Boys in Terre Haute, Indiana. After ten months Charles ran away—surprisingly, straight back to his mother! Kathleen wasn't about to lose her freedom, however, and she turned her son away.

Twelve-year-old Charles had finally gotten the message: He was on his own. To feed himself he stole—and quickly got caught. For the next seven years he was in and out of institutions: Indiana School for Boys, National Training School for Boys, Father Flanagan's Boy's Town, and the Federal Reformatory at Chillicothe, Ohio. By the age of 19, when he was granted parole from Chillicothe, Charles's offenses included armed robbery, car theft, a string of federal crimes, and homosexual rape.

Marriage at 20 failed to inspire a change in lifestyle. To support his new bride, Rosalie, Charles pulled off a series of burglaries. Then, in July of 1955, he and his now-pregnant wife headed for Los Angeles in a stolen

Mercury. Before the year was up, they were on their way east again, fleeing a five-year probation sentence. Charlie was tough to pin down, but the authorities finally caught up with him in Indianapolis, and he was returned to Los Angeles for trial. That escapade netted him a two-year sentence at Terminal Island Correctional Institution in San Pedro, California, with a concurrent five-year probation sentence tacked on when he tried to escape.

As I faced prisoner number 33465 in the small hearing room at Terminal Island, I felt a sense of dispair. Charles Miller Manson, the young man before me, had at age 23 never known a father, had been thrown out as a young teenager by his mother, had committed his first armed robbery at age 13, had never gone beyond the seventh grade, had never held a sustained job and, at this point, had spent over half his life in correctional institutions.

It wasn't just the sordid facts of Charlie's past that troubled me. The clinical evaluation and psychiatric study showed an alarming degree of hostility toward all authority and an extreme sex drive coupled with a hatred of all women. Manson's profile, combined with my conversation with him, added up to an overwhelming conclusion: Although his criminal record had for the most part consisted of bad checks, burglary, car theft, and pandering, Charles Miller Manson was indeed capable, because of his psychosexual confusion, of committing any crime necessary to achieve his abnormal sexual desires.

When the hearing was over, Charles Manson stood up and walked to the door. With a sense of foreboding I watched this five-foot-four-inch child-man. Slowly and deliberately he turned around and faced me: "Remember, Judge Reed, this time it was only a few bad checks and two cars." I assured him I was well aware of the charges.

He was almost out the door when he turned again, took

two steps toward me, and reiterated: "Be sure that you remember, Judge Reed, that I only took two cars on this bad rap." This time he was out the door and gone, but I couldn't help wondering whether case 33465 was trying to tell me there was worse to come.

Alone with my thoughts, I reviewed the total picture. It was always an awesome task to determine by the stroke of my pen the fate of another human being. But I had to bear in mind that there was always more than one human being involved; there were many out there beyond prison bars whose lives would be touched by the man or woman who walked free.

After wrestling with all the facts, the reports, and my own personal evaluation, I wrote my three-pronged conclusion. My finding of fact read that Charles Manson was, in my judgment, "a potential sex killer." My conclusion of law was that he should be "denied parole for the entire sentence." Finally, I warned the warden that the Board had concluded that Manson was an extremely dangerous criminal who should be kept under close custody until released. At that time I instructed the warden, that the County Sheriff and Police Chief of Los Angeles should be notified and fully apprised of the extremely dangerous nature of the criminal who was being released into their community.

On September 28, 1958, Charles Manson, having completed his full sentence, walked out of Terminal Island Prison a free man.

Charlie wasn't out long. During his two years of freedom he discovered his real calling. Increasingly in the late fifties the young, the disenchanted, and the rebellious were taking to the road to seek an ill-defined "freedom." Disengagement from family and social ties soon brought its own self-induced bondage, for the drifters had to eat. For young females it often meant turning to prostitution, the only profession available to them—and Charlie was there to give a helping hand and turn a profit for himself. For two years he "managed" a ragtag gaggle of teenage girls who seemed to recognize Charlie as an already-blossoming father figure and, ironically, a symbol of the authority which they had sacrificed so much to escape. Charlie was caught transporting girls across state lines for purposes of prostitution, and on June 23, 1960, he was sentenced to ten years at McNeil Island Federal Penitentiary.

McNeil was Charlie's graduate school in crime. Like a good student, he knew exactly what he wanted and he went for it. During the seven years of "hard time" that Manson actually served, he immersed himself in the study of magic, hypnotism, astral projection, subliminal motivation, Masonry, Scientology, ego games, and music. Hypnotism and subliminal motivation held a special fascination for him as a key to controlling other people for his own benefit. His seventh-grade education was no impediment as he devoured Dr. Eric Bernes's handbook of transactional analysis, *Games People Play*, or the basic tenets of Scientology under the tutelage of another inmate, "Dr. Lanier Royer". Charlie was determined to become the ultimate manipulator.

Music was also to play a major role in the life of the future self-styled "roving minstrel." It was Al Karpis, member of the bloody Ma Barker gang (responsible for 14 vicious murders), who taught Charlie steel guitar and much, much more. I had had a number of contacts with Karpis over the years, principally at Alcatraz, where he worked in the prison library. He habitually attempted to ingratiate himself with younger inmates and was known to exert a very negative influence on their conduct and attitude.

The music connection was to lead to Charles Manson's

ultimate delusion, the twisted philosophy that emerged as "Helter Skelter." It was Charlie's plan for world domination. The ideas which incubated during those seven years flowed as a confused mystical mix from two sources—the Bible and the lyrics of the Beatles. With the intensity of a newborn experience, Manson saw "Revolution 9" from the Beatle's "White Album" as a direct reference to Revelation chapter 9.

It was exciting, apocalyptic. Judgment would sweep the world in the last days, when, with blasting trumpet and falling stars, the smoking pit would release locusts and scorpions to torment the men of earth who did not bear the seal of God upon their foreheads. With what elation one can only imagine, Manson read that those avengers wore on their heads "crowns like gold, and their faces were as the faces of men." We don't know at what pace his philosophy matured, but we can picture the exhilaration when he came to the words, "And they had a king over them, which is the angel of the bottomless pit, whose name . . . is Apollyon."

In the dark recesses of his mind, Charles Manson recycled the Battle of Armageddon as a race war between the blacks and the affluent white middle class. But for Manson it was not in its ultimate outcome to be a racial reckoning. The victor would be narrowed to a band of followers . . . there would be a charismatic leader . . . they would take over the world . . . .

How far the scenario was fine-tuned at McNeil and later at Terminal Island before Manson's final release on March 21, 1967, we will never know. But one thing is certain: Never did Romans 1:21,22 seem more true: " . . . [they] became vain in their imaginations, and their foolish heart was darkened. Professing themselves to be wise, they became fools."

I lost track of Charles Manson until I was jolted to

recollection on October 15, 1969, by an Associated Press
release from *The San Francisco Examiner:*

> The last survivors of a band of nude and long-
> haired thieves who ranged over Death Valley
> in stolen dune buggies have been rounded up,
> the Sheriffs' office said yesterday. A Sheriffs'
> posse, guided by a spotter plane, arrested 27
> men and women members of the nomad band
> in two desert raids. Deputies said eight chil-
> dren, including two babies suffering from
> malnutrition, were also brought in. Some of the
> women were completely nude and others wore
> only bikini bottoms, deputies said. All the adults
> were booked at Inyo County Jail for investiga-
> tion of charges which included car theft, receiv-
> ing stolen property, and carrying illegal
> weapons. Six stolen dune buggies were recov-
> ered, deputies said.
>
> Deputy Sheriff Jerry Hildreth said the band
> lived off the land by stealing. He said they
> traveled in the stolen four-wheel-drive dune
> buggies and camped in a succession of aban-
> doned mining shacks. The band previously
> escaped capture by moving only at night and
> by setting up radio-equipped lookout posts on
> the mountains, he said. It was extraordinary the
> way they covered up their tracks and would
> make dummy camps to throw us off. Hildreth
> said they gave us a merry chase. . . . This is
> probably one of the most inaccessible areas in
> California.

Accompanying the bizarre newspaper accounts were
of course a number of pictures, including one of the

young man whom I had never been able to forget. Charlie had been discovered hiding in a tiny space beneath the sink of one of the desert shacks. From the newspaper accounts, Manson had obviously enlarged his operations. His prison university had served him well in preparing him for a leadership role.

Six weeks later, Manson's face was emblazoned upon the front pages of newspapers across the country. Now long-haired and wearing a wild scruff of beard, his eyes were nevertheless the same—glittering and hypnotic. Those eyes seemed to mock me as I recalled our last meeting: "...remember, Judge Reed, that I only took two cars on this bad rap." Now this man was the accused ringleader in the bloody Tate-La Bianca massacres in Los Angeles.

As the arraignment and trial unfolded, the world was treated at last to a full expose of the drop-out, tune-in, shoot-up generation of flower children and hippies. It could trace the descent of clean-cut, Sunday-school-going kids into the same hell-pit of depravity as the rejected sons and daughters of alcoholic and abusive parents. As an aunt of one of the girls involved was to say, "She couldn't do what they said she did in California. Patricia sang in the church choir and read the Bible." One of Manson's own followers would echo that belief when she declared, "I can't believe the stories they're telling about us. Charlie is such a warm and wonderful person."

In view of the evaluation I had written on Manson more than a dozen years before, I was more than interested in filling in the interval in order to see just how this "extremely dangerous young man" and "potential sex killer" had arrived at this milestone event in his criminal history.

San Francisco's Haight Ashbury district had become in the 1960's the mecca of America's disenchanted young.

It had in turn wrought its own enchantment. Cut loose from the restraints imposed by family and social conventions, the children of the 60's nevertheless sought a vaguely perceived chimera of reality, truth, freedom, and love. Pursued in a moral and a spiritual vacuum, those cravings all too often led by an easy descent to a false reality, a reinterpretation of truth, a moral and sometimes physical bondage, and exploitation instead of the longed-for love.

Especially for the girls. When they discovered Charlie, the bearded Christlike figure, the apostle of love, the guru whose wisdom was sufficient for all their own uncertainties, they flocked to become his disciples. Eventually he gathered 26 followers, 20 of them young women. A psychiatrist was later to characterize the girls as "hysterics, wishful thinkers, seekers after some absolute." Incredibly, few of them ever seemed aware that Manson was using them. Sexually exploited within the group, "loaned" out, intimidated into emotional dependence, most of them were fiercely loyal and proud of being "Charlie's girls."

When the Haight's mystique began to fade, the Manson "family" moved on, heading south for Los Angeles in an old VW bus. Here fast-talking Charlie got the elderly, blind owner of the Spahn Ranch (once a movie set and now a riding school, in the rocky foothills of the Santa Susanna Mountains) to agree, with the help of 5000 dollars of questionable origin, to allow the gang to stay. The isolated ranch was to be a "backside of the desert" period of preparation for the mission which Charlie had conceived at McNeil.

Drugs and girls continued to provide the modis operandi for Manson's domination of the group. The promise of easy drugs was often used to recruit members in the first place. The female newcomers were personally initiated by Charlie behind closed doors into the fine points of their particular contribution to the new community. The girls were thereafter forced to use their sexual favors to keep the men in line, whom they outnumbered four to one. An increasing cache of arms and ammunition further communicated the security of belonging and the folly of disassociating themselves. Charlie was never without his own symbol of authority, a conspicuously carried bowie knife.

In time, Los Angeles also soured for Manson. Rejected by two established musicians who failed to recognize anything marketable in his music, he began to fuel the bitter resentment toward the wealthy that had begun during his prison years. One of his contacts in the music world had gone so far as to invite him for an interview to the home in affluent Benedict Canyon which Sharon Tate and her husband were later to rent. The interview led nowhere, but Manson now clearly saw where fate had decreed that Armageddon should begin.

Charlie's vision of that event had become crystal clear. He as king would direct a bloodbath to be unleashed on the white people of Los Angeles, people whom he termed "pigs" and unworthy to live. This in turn would trigger the opportunity for revenge which the blacks were looking for. To escape the genocide that would ensue, Charlie and his Family would flee to a remote and impregnable hideaway prepared in advance in the Mohave Desert. As Manson's vast ego saw it, however, the blacks would lack the know-how to reorder society after the killing stopped. That's when he and his followers would emerge to establish their kingdom.

The preparation of the desert redoubt was a task seriously pursued. An avid admirer of General Rommel, Hitler's sly "Desert Fox" of the Africa campaign, Manson began "collecting" a fleet of VW's, stripping them down, and converting them into a brigade of armored dune buggies. Some were fitted with gun mounts.

The network of roads and byways and negotiable wilderness became familiar terrain to Manson and his followers. Fire roads were no impediment. They sawed off the locks and replaced them with their own. In strategic places they hid caches of food and arms. In countless rehearsals, the fleet of vehicles laid a twisting network of tracks several hundred miles long to the dilapidated shacks of their desert "fortress," the Barker Ranch. Golden-tongued Charlie Manson had talked its owner, a wealthy Los Angeles widow, into letting "The Family" take over.

The stage was set. Helter Skelter's time had come. Strangely enough, the charismatic and authoritarian leader of this motley band was not to lead his troops into battle. He saw himself as initiator, energizer, evil genius— not as general. Four advance troops were sent that August 9th of 1969 to spark Armageddon—Charles "Tex" Watson, age 24, all-American boy turned on to LSD; Linda Kasabian, 20, ethereal, twice-married, and a relative newcomer; Susan Atkins, 21, and daughter of alcoholic parents and Patricia Krenwinkel, also 21, and a former choir member. Linda, as the newest recruit, drove. All of them were high on LSD, all wore black, and all of them were armed as they pulled in to the targeted mansion in Benedict Canyon.

The next morning when police arrived, even they were horrified by what they saw. On the lawn lay two bodies, one gunned down, the other repeatedly stabbed. In a nearby car a third body bearing three bullet wounds lay dead on the seat. Inside the house were two more bodies. One of them was actress Sharon Tate, 8½ months pregnant and married to the well-known Polish film director Roman Polanski, who was then in London. Police counted 16 stab wounds in her upper torso. On the door, written in her blood, was the word "Pig."

Back at the Ranch, Manson welcomed the troops home. Four girls and one man had done away with five of the hated "pigs" in one night. But the job had been messy, and Manson wanted a quick follow-up on how to do it right. This time wealthy retired grocer Leno La Bianca and his wife Rosemary were the victims. The scene when the police arrived was as grisly as the night before. Head covered with a white bag, Leno lay with a carving fork protruding from his chest. His wife had been repeatedly stabbed. "Death to pigs" was traced in blood on the white enamel of the refrigerator door.

One week later all the derelicts at the Spahn Ranch, including Manson, were in custody—and released. Despite the stolen vehicles, the guns, and the juvenile runaways that the raid netted, they couldn't be held even on those counts for "the lack of evidence."

In the murky recesses of Manson's mind, he fully expected the Armageddon he had fused to sweep Los Angeles and the country in all its fury. When it didn't, he nevertheless pulled up stakes and retreated to the Barker Ranch, just a mile or two south of the Death Valley National Monument. Disappointed in seeing his prophetic utterances remain unfulfilled, Charlie still found much to fuel his fantasies. The desert-dwellers surrounding them were now the enemy. There was much talk in the evenings of terrorizing and taking over isolated Death Valley communities, of paralyzing the effectiveness of the police—and worse. Members were provided with knives and instructed in their most vicious use. They would boil the skulls of their victims in vats and display their trophies around the ranch. Clearly the craving to kill had not been satiated by the blood orgy in Los Angeles.

Meanwhile the police were in a frenzy of activity. It is estimated that 8750 detective hours were spent in unraveling the case. Still, the law didn't close in on the holed-up Family until a minor complaint sent the Highway Patrol to investigate. The presence of so many vehicles led to further incursions by the police and the raid which culminated in the booking of Manson and nine others on two counts of receiving stolen property.

Manson's arrest was at this point in no way connected to the Tate-La Bianca massacre. Most of his followers had scattered, and the case didn't break until a few months after the murders, when jailhouse "canary" Susan Atkins sang while locked up on another charge. Linda Kasabian, offered immunity for her testimony on behalf of the prosecution, provided the eyewitness evidence that was needed to indict Manson and his accomplices. The others named were picked up from here and there around the country, including Leslie Van Houten, who had been present only at the La Bianca killings.

The trial began in June of 1970 and lasted a record 129 days, the longest murder trial in California history. When it was over Charles Manson, Tex Watson, Susan Atkins, Patricia Krenwinkel, and Leslie Van Houten had been convicted of first-degree murder. Manson had been committed to a psychiatric institution prior to the proceedings, but joined the rest on death row after the penalty phase of the trial was completed.

Incredible as it may seem, Charles Manson had his champions. They ranged all the way from news-starved journalists of the "yellow press," to fellow members of the counterculture (who saw in him a legitimate rebel), to sincere and kindly souls who found it hard to look beyond the pitiful ingredients of the condemned man's childhood. Finally, there were those who believed that no crime, no matter how heinous, warranted the supreme penalty.

The sympathy, the protests, the philosophical arguments became superfluous when in February of 1972 the California Supreme Court declared the death penalty unconstitutional. Thus, at a stroke of the pen, all convicts on death row had their sentences automatically changed to life imprisonment.

Charlie Manson has spent most of the last 16 years of his life in solitary confinement. That isolation is protective rather than punitive. Even the prison underworld has its way of exacting "justice" within its ranks.

Rehabilitation has played no part in the long, lonely years at Folsom, Vacaville, and San Quentin. Increasingly, the dreams and the visions have become the prisoner's only reality.

Charles Manson most recently came to public attention when he made his sixth unsuccessful bid for parole. Still the philosopher, he began reading from a sheaf of papers a long and incoherent recital. There was talk of visiting the Ayatollah.

Most chilling of all was Manson's reference to what he viewed as the crowning achievement of his life's work. "From the world of darkness, I did loose demons and devils in the power of scorpions to torment." His original apocalyptic vision based upon Revelation 9 was still intact.

This was not the kind of recital to incline the three-member panel to view his bid for parole optimistically. It took them a scant 30 minutes to declare this "caged, vicious, wild animal" (as Prosecutor Stephen Kay described him before the panel) unfit for parole.

As the case of Charlie Manson and his "Family" recede further and further from the public memory, I am impelled to view him not as an isolated aberration of the human condition, or even as the symbol of the rootless and disorientated of a particular era, but as an example in microcosm of the rebellion that lies in the heart of every human being. Charlie wanted desperately to be in control. Charlie rewrote for his disciples all the standards of right and wrong. Indeed, at his trial he told reporters, "I have no guilt. You can't judge me. Only I can judge me."

But it wasn't the enormity of Charles Manson's crime that separated him from God. It was his rebellious and unrepentant heart. And so it is with many people today: Vain in their imagination, with foolish and darkened hearts, they repent not, as Revelation 9:21 puts it, "of their murders, nor of their sorceries, nor of their fornication, nor of their thefts." So it has been with Charles Miller Manson.

14
Youth in Revolt

Let no man despise thy youth; but be thou an example of the believers in word, in conversation, in charity, in spirit, in faith, in purity.

Protest has been a part of the human condition ever since Satan implanted the first challenge to the Creator's authority in Eve's mind. The tempter's "Hath God said?" opened to question God's one and only "thou shalt not" imposed on the innocent pair in their garden paradise. Having partaken of the forbidden fruit, our first parents eyed with wonder the choices for good and evil open to them. In his unregenerate condition, man is still looking with yearning upon the forbidden and is still chafing under the bonds of law and of social order.

The sixties were a unique era in our nation's history, for "protest" took on the proportions of a cult exercise. It was a decade that saw the generation gap become a painful and lingering reality for millions of families. It was a time of revolt against the agencies of law; "pig" became the accepted designation for the enforcers of neighborhood peace. It was a time of violence in the urban ghetto, where the raised fist became the all-too-well-understood symbol of black power. It was also the time of the flower children, those visionary apostles of love with their gentle rebuke of all who failed to look at life's complexities through the drooping petals of a bloom. It was the time of Haight Ashbury and the hippies, who rejected the material world of their elders and opted for an inward and an otherworldly quest through drugs.

Most significantly, it was the Vietnam War which brought together the many segments of a confused and alienated society. The process was not simple. Clearly, a great many people were questioning the value structure they had until then accepted as American and therefore "right." Its tenets were straightforward: Our prosperity was the result of the American work ethic; our technology was always utilized in the public interest; our system of democracy was a gift to humanity, and it was our responsibility to export it. The challenges to these tenets became an exercise in simplistic logic, and in the absence of an absolute and divinely ordained morality, authored by a transcendent God, the modus operandi must be a destructive one.

Through the same metamorphosis by which Adam blamed God for his own decision to join in Eve's act of disobedience ("The woman whom thou gavest to be with me, she gave me of the tree, and I did eat"), so now a very audible segment of the American public labeled an impersonal "society" the culprit for all its individual failures and shortcomings. Hence, society itself must be destroyed. It was immoral. It was obscene. It was irredeemable. That conclusion was an act of mental gymnastics that had recurred again and again throughout man's history—this neat escape from a personal accountability to God to a generalized fixation of blame upon "society."

The "destruction of society" was the fundamental tenet of the radical left, and that belief sifted down by easy stages to a receptive youth population for whom "radical," "change," and "antiestablishment" became readily assimilable catchwords.

There was no lack of idealism embodied in the lust for destruction. As the leader of the radical left candidly explained, the axe was to be laid to the evil root of the establishment's institutions so that out of the chaos a more beneficent society could emerge. The hot-eyed activist, whether at Berkeley or Columbia or Ohio State, demanded freedom to pursue arson, to destroy federal property, and to take over university administrative buildings with impunity. When asked, "What do you propose in place of what you have destroyed?" the answer was a cryptic "The battle is itself the object." With even more chilling ambivalence, Tom Hayden, when asked in a public debate to clarify his revolutionary program, responded, "We haven't any. First we will make the revolution, and then we will find out what for." Clearly there was small intellectual demand made upon the revolutionary masses of the sixties!

As the war escalated, the emotional rather than intellectual content of the new radicalism gave rise to a soon-to-become-familiar set of emotive buzz words and phrases: "*Fascist* America, run by the *military-industrial complex,* is waging an *immoral* war against the *peoples* of Vietnam and thus committing an *obscene* act of *genocide.*" It was a denouncement that rolled easily from the lips of the antiwar protesters. That there were facts and issues to be rationally discussed was lost in the rhetoric.

From there it was an easy step to the accommodation

that Mary McCarthy expressed in a *New York Review of Books* article entitled "On Withdrawing From Vietnam: An Exchange": "The alternatives to Communism offered by the Western countries are all ugly in their own ways and getting uglier. What I would hope for politically is an internal evolution in the Communist states toward greater freedom and plurality of choice." No matter that this "greater freedom" had not been a distinguishing mark of the Communist system. No matter that such a "hope" had never yet been realized. Students on America's campuses waved as enthusiastically as any Hanoi youth the little Red Book of Mao's sayings. "Let a thousand flowers bloom," it declared, in hyped reference to the happy coexistence of countless contradictory political ideas. But on those same pages Mao called for "death to the imperialists and their running dogs," and America's students mouthed both sentiments with equal enthusiasm. George Orwell, astute exposer of totalitarianism in all its insidious forms, said it well:

> There is a minority of intellectual pacifists whose real though unadmitted motive appears to be hatred of Western democracy and admiration of totalitarianism. . . . If one looks closely at the writings of the younger intellectual pacifists, one finds that they do not by any means express impartial disapproval but are directed almost entirely against Britain and the United States. Moreover they do not as a rule condemn violence as such, but only violence used in defense of Western Countries.*

---

* *The Radical Left*, edited by William P. Gerberding and Duane E. Smith (Houghton Mifflin Co., 1970), p. 66.

U.S. involvement in the Vietnam War came at this most inauspicious time in American history. Few would argue that when the war first broke out, American sympathies were with the people of South Vietnam, who, like the North Vietnamese, had been newly freed of French control, but who did not wish to be reunited with a Communistic sister-state. We sent advisers to help. It seemed the decent thing, the very "American" thing to do. But as the years went by and the small group of advisers turned to a swelling stream of armed troops committed to a never-declared war, the protests grew. It had become apparent that a "limited war" could not win the struggle. Those who had initially been in favor of our involvement saw no easy way out of our commitment.

My own involvement with the war-protest movement of the sixties and seventies centered upon my parole dealings with young Selective Service violators. One morning a few weeks after resuming my post with the U.S. Board of Parole in Washington D.C., my secretary informed me that an important visitor was waiting to see me. Though he had no appointment, he insisted that he had come to my office on urgent business and must have an audience at once.

A few minutes later Dr. Willard Gaylin introduced himself. He was, he said, a psychoanalyst at the Columbia University Clinic and a professor at Union Theological Seminary. He further informed me that the Director of the Federal Bureau of Prisons, Myril Alexander, had two years previously given him permission to interview Selective Service violators and to review their files in order to gain information for a book he was then in the process of writing.

It seemed that Dr. Gaylin's interest in the subject had

first developed from a philosophical point of view. "But," declared Gaylin, "I hadn't yet met these young men. I hadn't seen the walls of a prison. I hadn't measured the brevity of time in which youth can be lost and hope abandoned. I came as an observer and left as a participant."

Dr. Gaylin had indeed became a participant, because after spending two years interviewing the Federal Bureau of Prison's Selective Service inmates and researching their files, he spent a culminating 45 minutes of angry confrontation with me, challenging the U.S. Board of Parole's policies and procedures relative to these young men. Then, looking very much pleased with himself at having confirmed his preconceived notions, he took his farewell, declaring that with this final material his book was now ready to go to press.

I looked forward to its publication with somewhat nervous anticipation. About nine months later, *In the Service of Their Country* was in the bookstores. I noted with interest that the burden of virtually the entire book was a defense of Selective Service violators in the sixties, whom Gaylin described as "philosophical objectors" to the war in Vietnam. On the other hand, he was very critical of the U.S. Parole Board's policy of granting earlier releases to "conscientious objectors," whose long-held moral and religious convictions that all wars were wrong prohibited them from taking up arms. He found it repugnant that we paroled young Jehovah's Witnesses much earlier than youths who rioted and rampaged on college campuses. I had explained to him that most of the adherents to this sect had formed their belief systems while very young and were only carrying out their life-long convictions. Most of the young college radicals, however, had only recently discovered their "consciences" and had found it timely to "object" when they became eligible for the draft.

As I read on, it became clearer and clearer what Dr. Gaylin had had in mind on that unannounced visit. He had, I recalled, asked to see a profile on each member of the Parole Board. His written comment in the book was, "The profiles were obviously made out by the members themselves because they varied greatly in the amount of information offered. Because we live in an age where issues of color are not to be ignored, where the volatility of our society and the sensitivity of our people demand its constant consideration, I asked Chairman Reed how many members of the Board were black. He indicated that traditionally during his administration there always had been one black member of the Parole Board but that the black member's term of office had expired and he personally had decided not to recommend his reappointment (why, he did not say)."

The implication was damaging to the image of the Parole Board, but the facts were quite otherwise and had been accurately relayed at our conference as follows. Upon returning to the Parole Board as Chairman in May 1969, I had conducted a nationwide search to secure the best-qualified black person to fill the vacancy of retiree Homer Benson. We had found such a person in the very-well-qualified Honorable Curtis C. Crawford of Saint Louis, Missouri. It was not, however, until after Dr. Gaylin's book came out that Curtis Crawford, along with a highly qualified woman, Paula Terment of California, were sworn in as our new Parole Board members. Both were to serve with great distinction over a period of many years. So much for objective reporting.

The Selective Service violators whom Dr. Gaylin and others like him sought to cast in the role of martyrs had two very vocal champions in the brothers Berrigan. For their activities, they too came under the jurisdiction of the Federal Parole Board. The two Catholic priests made headlines for years by defying both church and government in a series of attacks on Selective Service offices.

Phillip first made news in October of 1967 when he walked into the Baltimore Selective Service office and poured blood over the draft registration cards stored there. He had not yet been incarcerated for that offense when he and his brother Daniel boldly removed draft registration records from the files of the Catonsville, Maryland, Selective Service office. They carried these outside, poured homemade napalm over them, and intoned the Lord's Prayer as they watched them burn to ashes. For this audacious destruction of federal property, Daniel was sentenced to three years in prison and Phillip to 3 ½ years, to run concurrently with his prior sentence.

The burning of the draft cards gave the Berrigan brothers the media attention they needed to establish themselves as the cult leaders of the protest movement. The trial itself became a means of further fixing the halo of martyrdom upon their brows. When the verdict was pronounced, they again bowed their heads and repeated the Lord's Prayer.

Phillip and Daniel Berrigan's martyr roles were seriously flawed, however, when neither showed up on April 9, 1970, to begin their prison terms. A manhunt ensued. Phillip was taken about two weeks later. Daniel eluded capture until August. Imprisoned at last, they each continued their now-wholesale denunciations and activist roles against "the system." Phillip organized fellow inmates at Lewisburg Federal Prison to rebel against the "injustices" of their incarceration, while Daniel did the same at Danbury Federal Prison. There he incited a riot that endangered the lives of both prison officials and inmates.

Little wonder that we felt compelled to turn down their

applications for parole, a move that elicited a well-publicized but ineffective hunger strike. They are out now, and they no doubt feel that the words Daniel wrote in prison are still as apropos today as then: ". . . the war goes on. We are locked up for the duration paying tribute with our lives to a system of crime and punishment that punishes the crime of peacefulness and refuses to indict the crime of war." Perhaps it is through different eyes that men like the brothers Berrigan view the present fruits of "peace" in Cambodia and Afghanistan.

The year 1971 was to see a concerted attempt on the part of antiwar protesters to bring the federal government to its knees. It was cherry blossom time in Washington, and the 50,000 people who had gathered at the George Washington Monument to applaud the speeches of the appeasers broke ranks to make a frenzied assault on the White House barricades.

The mob's main target, however, was the Department of Justice, which they attacked in an attempt to destroy the files of FBI Chief J. Edgar Hoover, the hated symbol of law and order. Our intelligence-gathering capability had not yet been so impinged by acts of Congress as was later to be the case, and the Justice Department was accurately apprised of the time and the place of the attack. Within the building, battalions of Marines, along with Army and Air Force personnel, had been stationed ready to meet the emergency.

When two demonstrators made a dash for the flagpole in front of the Justice Department and hoisted the Communist flag of North Vietnam, the melee began. The police and specially trained militia in full battle gear poured out of the building to protect its records and the security of the nation.

It was hardly an overreaction. The Parole Board had a number of times been forced to adjourn meetings and vacate the building because of bomb threats. Only a few days before the assault on the Justice Department, a terrorist gang had planted a bomb in a room in the Capitol Building, causing great damage but fortunately no fatalities. The President and Secretary of Defense had wisely called in thousands of militia to safeguard federal buildings, access roads, communications systems, and key government personnel.

The morning of the second day of the siege I was driving down Massachusetts Avenue en route to my office when, short of Du Pont Circle, I noted that an angry crowd of young demonstrators had broken through police lines. They surged across the intersection, stopping traffic and shouting, "Stop the war! Stop the government!" When they began attempting to overturn the automobiles of government executives on their way to their offices, I became alarmed. If they discovered my identity, my life could well be in danger. The car ahead was just rolling over when three companies of Marines in full battle gear came charging down on the students and drove them back toward Georgetown. My hands were sweaty as I relaxed my death grip on the steering wheel. "Thank You. Thank You, Lord," I breathed.

The incident heightened the sense of tragedy I felt in the days to come. I thought of the pinnacle of power from which we had fallen since VJ Day, when General Douglas MacArthur had accepted the surrender of the Japanese aboard the *U.S.S. Missouri* in Tokyo Bay, thus ending World War II. I was convinced that some of the reasons for America's fall from her lofty position surely lay in the files of the Alger Hiss case, as reviewed by the Parole Board of the United States. In 1945 he had sat by the side of ailing President Roosevelt at the Yalta Conference, where Western Europe was divided up and an iron curtain drawn across the continent. Two months later, as chief organizer of the United Nations and Andrei Gromyko's choice as its temporary Secretary General, Hiss was in San Francisco. I had always believed that much more than perjury had been at stake in the Hiss case.

Our halfhearted approaches to "limited warfare" in Korea and later South Vietnam infused the military and civilian population with a negative philosophy, which resulted in our humiliating defeat in South Vietnam.

The "undeclared war" continues, but now it is waged against the fundamental principles of democratic hopes worldwide. Iran, once a staunch friend and solidly on the path of sociological, educational, and economic reform, has slipped back into a frenzied dark age of hatred and bigotry. Taken hostage in our own embassy in Tehran, 52 Americans came to know only too well during the 444 days they were locked up how far the United States had sunk in the world's esteem. And when the Soviet Union by military force crushed Afghanistan and executed its President, the weak protests of our State Department scarcely registered.

Today, when Central American terrorists, armed with both Cuban and Soviet weapons, seek to overthrow democratic governments and establish Communist puppet dictatorships, our myopic citizens mount vociferous protests—but not against the usurpers. Their target is President Reagan and his efforts to get military and economic aid to those countries opposed to a Communist takeover in Central America.

Granted, there is a resurgence of patriotic fervor in the present decade, yet the fallout of the sixties is still felt. But misguided as they were, the radical activists who shouted for the overthrow of their government in those "days of rage" at least *thought* they were serving the cause of humanity. Today's traitors are more likely to betray their country's secrets for monetary gain.

What do those once-young idealists of the sixties think when they consider the closing words of North Vietnam's victor, Ho Chi Minh, in a speech given in 1960?

> Our party is as great as the immense sea, the high mountain. It has won so much love in thirty years of struggle and success. Our Party is virtue, civilization, unity, independence, a peaceful and comfortable life.
>
> Its acts of kindness and service are really great. Its thirty-year history is a whole garden book of history.
>
> Long live the great Viet-Nam Worker's Party!
>
> Long live a peaceful, unified, independent, democratic, prosperous, and strong Viet-Nam!
>
> Long live the socialist community headed by the great Soviet Union!
>
> Long live Communism!
>
> Long live world peace!

What do they think, in view of the bloodbath that finally "pacified" Cambodia or the lingering death that has been imposed by Russian troops on the people of Afghanistan? A *Los Angeles Times* news release dated February 27, 1986, stated the grim facts:

> Soviet troops in Afghanistan killed about 35,000 civilians last year in a campaign of "systematic brutality" that included bombing villages and planting explosives in children's toys, a report prepared for the U.N. Human Rights commission said.

It is not only beyond our borders that the threat lies. Do we really understand the implications of the 1981 arrest of two fugitive veterans of the radical left of the 1960's, Katherine Boudine and Judith Clark? They were apprehended in connection with a million-dollar Brinks armored car holdup and charged along with two more companions with the murders of two policemen. Boudine's and Clark's arrest led to the "terrorist connection" and the discovery of a bomb factory, arms caches, safe houses, the floor plans of a Queens County criminal court, and possible assassination lists.

Today we live not only with the constant threat of terrorism directed against our citizens when they venture into the air or onto foreign shores. We must even live (and perhaps someday die) with the grim knowledge that some of our fellow Americans, who have the same rights and liberties as we do, are plotting to bring down a nation which to most of the world is still mankind's last and only hope.

"A prudent man foreseeth the evil and fleeth from it," warned Solomon. We would do well to take a long, instructive look at the many closed doors and impregnable walls of Eastern Europe, and then commit ourselves again to defend with all our physical and moral capabilities the benefits and blessings with which God has so graciously gifted us!

15
Corruption and the Mob

Fret not thyself because . . . of the man who
bringeth wicked devices to pass . . .
For evildoers shall be cut off, but those that
wait upon the Lord shall inherit the earth.

It is little wonder that the youth of the sixties were
caught up in a philosophy of rebellion and lawlessness.
The more obvious rationale for their destructive activities lay in the cruelties of war, in racial discrimination,
in the inequities of economic status. But beyond that was
another reason: Their elders were setting a horrific
example, an example that claimed no philosophical base,
no neat humanitarian "cause" that would justify the
overthrow of a deficient society, no political platform
no matter how vaguely formulated. The sins of their
fathers were all too often sheer greed and lust for power.
During the decade of the sixties a crime wave of
gigantic proportions swept across America. According to
the Federal Bureau of Investigation's *Uniform Crime*

Report, violent crimes such as murder, rape, robbery, and aggravated assault nearly tripled between 1960 and 1976. Even more ominous than escalating crime on the streets and in the neighborhoods, however, was the rise of a sinister network of well-organized criminal dynasties that attempted to put a stranglehold on free and honest American enterprise. No businessman or politician was immune if the mob deemed that by coercion or bribery or graft it could bring yet another source of revenue under the control of its evil empire.

The Mafia, as the organization and its related branches was called, was of Sicilian origin. It was run as a "family" business, but its true bloodlines were based on an unbreakable code of loyalty and silence. Vengeance was swift and inexorable for those who didn't observe the rules. On the other hand, the rewards for politicians and law-enforcement agencies who cooperated were incredibly sweet. Thus it was that mobster Frank Costello had a free hand in running New York's infamous Tammany Hall gang of politicians for the better part of 50 years, while the underworld gangster Al Capone was able to establish with impunity his unholy alliance with the city fathers of Chicago and claim that city as his royal fief.

It was in the early fifties that Congress first began investigating the suspected menace of organized crime. Hearings presided over by Senator Estes Kefauver established beyond a doubt that a national crime syndicate did indeed exist. The Kefauver Committee reported the ominous facts:

> These criminal gangs possessed such power and had access to such sources of protection that they constituted a government within a government in this country . . . a government by the underworld. . . .

This phantom government nevertheless enforces its own law, carries out its own executions, and not only ignores but abhors the democratic processes of justice which are held to be the safeguards of the American citizen.

This secret government of crimesters is a serious menace which could, if not curbed, become the basis for a subversive movement which could wreck the very foundations of this country.

In the early sixties the Mafia came under the close scrutiny of the Senate Permanent Subcommittee on Investigations and the Senate Select Committee on Improper Activites in the Labor and Management Field. Both were chaired by my good friend of 25 years, Senator John L. McClellan of Arkansas. As investigators for the committees continued looking into organized crime, the shadowy undercurrents of the Mafia began to take more tangible shape.

In the process of reviewing the Mafia's long history in the evidence uncovered by the FBI, the Federal Bureau of Narcotics, and the Department of Justice's Organized Crime Unit, as well as in the devastating testimony of Joseph Valachi (a longtime New York hoodlum who dared to break the mob's code of silence), I detected an ominous pattern that would become all too familiar when I had to deal personally with the racketeers of my own day. The all-time king of syndicated crime was undisputably Al Capone, but the crown prince was his successor, Paul Ricca, alias "The Waiter." Capone and his henchmen were clever enough never to become involved in crimes of impulse or passion. Their moves were professional, with all risks anticipated.

Ricca was equally as wily. He came to the U.S. from

Italy in 1920, a fugitive from justice on a murder charge. His first ten years were an apprenticeship—falsification of identity papers, extortion, postal fraud, conspiracy, and income tax evasion—all the coursework prerequisite to leadership in the mob. He had a dozen arrests to his credit by the time he became a top syndicate leader on a national scale in the mid-thirties.

In 1941 Ricca, along with a number of other mobsters, was charged with a million-dollar extortion scheme. Ricca, sentenced to ten years in the federal penitentiary in Atlanta, but paroled after only four, had boasted that he had connections in the White House and ordered his lawyers to provide "money, favors, a seat in the Supreme Court" or whatever was necessary to the man who could get him out. This entire situation occurred some eight years before my appointment to the United States Board of Parole.

The easy parole and the braggadocio that accompanied it infuriated the press, and Ricca's case became a national scandal. Public embarrassment didn't prevent him from taking control of the Chicago Mob in the late 1940's, a position he held until his death in 1972, except for a brief retirement period in the mid-sixties when the government was investigating him for income tax evasion, and inaugurated deportation proceedings.

Ricca was loath to leave the good life, and he and his lawyers convinced Italy he was an undesirable character (not a difficult procedure in view of all the readily available news releases), while at the same time they were trying to convince the U.S. government that he was an upstanding and gainfully employed citizen. In fact, neither the United States nor the approximately 60 countries to which Ricca was allowed to appeal for sanctuary wanted him, especially after leafing through the lurid news clippings that Ricca's lawyers always helpfully enclosed with his application. Eventually he was success-fully convicted of income tax evasion and sentenced to nine more years in federal prison and given a token fine. In October 1961, after serving a little over two years, Ricca was freed, though not by the Parole Board. He was never deported and died a natural death in 1972.

The lesson was clear: It had been no idle boast that Ricca had influence where it counted. As I reviewed the cases of other prominent underworld figures, the pattern held. Money was power, and by means of bribes, extortion, payoffs, murder—every conceivable use of unbridled influence—the Mob was running a considerable segment of the American scene. Even when legal ploys failed and the godfathers of the underworld took a brief break in prison, they were often able to continue sending the orders that kept their empires functioning smoothly on the outside.

As Senator John McClellan and his team continued probing the inner working of the Mafia, they soon uncovered a close relationship between organized crime and some of the giants in the labor movement. At this time the leader of the Teamsters, the largest and most powerful of the labor unions, was James Riddle Hoffa, epitome of all that was corrupt and sinister. I had often seen him at Washington functions, and because the marble palace of the International Brotherhood of Team-sters Headquarters building was only a block from the Parole Board offices at First and Indiana, I had often met him and his bodyguards taking a walk after lunch.

Hoffa's ascent to the pinnacle of power had been ruthless and had involved either as protagonists or enemies some of our nation's most prominent public figures. According to Ed Partin, a former Hoffa aide who agreed to talk in return for immunity from prosecution, the lines of loyalty between Hoffa and Nixon had been firmly established as far back as 1960, during Nixon's unsuccessful presidential campaign against John Kennedy. It was fear of Kennedy rather than love of Nixon that led Hoffa to contribute an alleged half-million dollars toward the Nixon campaign. It was a low price, apparently, to keep his sworn enemy Robert Kennedy from being appointed Attorney General if his brother won.

Also illustrative of Jimmy Hoffa's activities was the five million dollars of Teamster pension funds he invested in Las Vegas's most glamorous gambling casino, Caesar's Palace. Eventually he was to up his original investment to over 50 million dollars, representing loans to five more hotels, a hospital, two golf courses, and other gangster-oriented enterprises. Rumor had it that the take on "skimming" (the taking of unreported profits) totaled six million dollars in one year in six Las Vegas casinos. Governor Sawyer's instructions to investigate, however, led only to halfhearted and inconclusive hearings. Suspicion gave way to action when federal officials presented evidence of skimming before the U.S. Grand Jury in May, 1967, and seven Las Vegas Strip officials were indicted for conspiring to divert money from gaming profits in order to evade corporate income taxes. To the outrage of the news media, the public, and the Justice Department's Organized Crime and Racketeering Division, all charges were subsequently dismissed. My colleague, Henry E. Petersen, the chief of the latter organization, was not in fact aware that the case had been dismissed until it was all over.

The dismay registered by the Crime and Racketeering Division's chief and by Mitchell Rogovin, Assistant Attorney General in charge of the tax division, can well be imagined. Having served with these two gentlemen within the Department of Justice over a period of many years, I have great respect for both their ability and their complete integrity. I have often wondered who in the federal government was responsible for sending out the order to drop charges against the big casino operators. Law enforcement officials in Nevada and the nation's capital freely expressed off-the-record opinions that the Johnson White House made the political decision to keep hands off in Las Vegas.

When the Mafia has such enormous power that they can control decision-making at the highest levels of government, and when labor unions are allowed to invest millions of dollars of the citizens' money in Nevada gambling casinos, it is little wonder that our nation's youth refuse to respect its representatives in government.

Wily as Hoffa was, he was not so fortunate as some of his brother hoodlums. On March 12, 1964, he was handed down an eight-year adult indeterminate sentence for jury tampering. In passing sentence, Judge Frank W. Wilson addressed these words to the Teamsters' president:

> You stand here convicted of seeking to corrupt the administration of justice itself. . . . of having tampered, really, with the very soul of this nation . . . because without a fair, proper and a lawful administration of justice, nothing else would be possible in this country—the administration of labor unions, the administration of business, the carrying on of recreation, the administration of health services, everything that we call civilization depends ultimately upon the proper administration of justice itself.
>
> Now, if a conviction of such an offense were to go unpunished and this type of conduct and this type of offense permitted to pass without

action by the Court, it would surely destroy
this country more quickly and more surely than
any combination of any foreign foes that we
could ever possibly have.*

As a result of much legal maneuvering, Hoffa did not
begin serving his time until three years later, on March
7, 1967. Two years into his term of imprisonment, he
received a consecutive five-year sentence for mail and
wire fraud. His case was scheduled to come before the
United States Board of Parole in October of 1969, one
third of the way through his eight-year term.

When the session began, on October 2, the Parole
Board urgently requested information from the Justice
Department on Hoffa's degree of involvement in organized crime. Our request went unheeded. We were
convinced, however, that jury tampering and mail
fraud were only the tip of the iceberg, and, acting on
confidential information from a former member of the
organized crime section of the Justice Department and
other informants, we denied Hoffa parole and continued
his case to March 1971. In his monumental study of the
Hoffa affair, Walter Sheridan, former special assistant to
Attorney General Robert F. Kennedy, explained:

Now the only avenue open for Hoffa's release
before that time [March 1971] was a commu-
tation of his sentence by the President of the
United States. The exploration of this possibility
had already begun at the White House.‡

---

* Walter Sheridan, *The Fall and Rise of Jimmy Hoffa* (Saturday Review Press, 1972), p. 355.

‡ Ibid., p. 467.

The subtle pressures began. It was a familiar process by now, but in Hoffa's case events took an ominous turn. There were hints from top officials that the paroling of Hoffa could be "one of the greatest decisions of my life." At first I didn't take them too seriously. Certainly I didn't respond to them. I left unspoken my question as to whether the one accosting me meant that Hoffa should be paroled on moral grounds or because my professional future was at stake.

The picture came into sharp focus in mid-February 1971, as I was catching an early-morning flight from Washington to Detroit to address a Federal Judicial Conference. To my surprise, I found myself seated next to a high-ranking official in the Justice Department, who had obviously requested this seat for a purpose. He lost no time in coming right to the point.

"Judge Reed, just what would you require of Jimmy Hoffa before you'd consider parole? What would he have to do to get out?" I deliberately ignored the deeper implications of such a question.

As always, when probed concerning parole possibilities, I made it clear that such matters were *Board* and not *individual* decisions. I did explain, off the record, however, that among the necessary prerequisites for parole, I personally would want to see Hoffa resign the presidency of the Teamsters and thus relinquish all authority over its pension funds, and also to cut all contact with organized crime figures.

His response startled me. "[Attorney General] John Mitchell has asked me to negotiate with you for Hoffa's speedy release."

Such boldness was shocking. Does one negotiate *justice*? Hoffa's next parole hearing was scheduled for the following month. The implication that I could be

bought angered me. "Sir," I responded, "I've been
around here a long time and dealt with the White House
and any number of attorneys general on important parole
cases, and I've never, to date, *negotiated* any decision
of the Board with the Attorney General or anyone else.
I don't intend altering that policy in this case."

"But this is important, George. Very, *very* important.
We've got to see that Nixon's reelected in '72. You know
that."

I agreed on the importance of the Nixon reelection,
but not on the necessity of Hoffa's release to achieve that
goal, and made that very clear. Nothing further was said
on that subject during the remainder of the flight.

A few days later, however, I was asked to meet with
this same official in his office. Again I was treated to a
very serious lecture on how vital Hoffa's release was to
the outcome of the upcoming election.

"You're improperly injecting yourself into the prov-
ince of the Parole Board, I responded bluntly. "This
hearing—like all others—must remain free of politics."
I couldn't say it more plainly.

"By the way," I added, "while I'm here I'd like to
renew my request for a copy of the Criminal Division's
'Epstein Report.' "

This crucial memorandum had been written just before
Mike Epstein's departure from the Justice Department.
As Walter Sheridan explained:

> Epstein's memorandum set forth the efforts
> that had been made during the previous seven
> years to keep Hoffa from going to prison and
> subsequently to obtain his release. . . . [Epstein]
> attached another memorandum suggesting that
> [the information] be referred to the Parole

> Board for its consideration.
> The memorandum went to [Criminal Division Director] Will Wilson but it was never sent to the Parole Board. It was sent instead to the files.*

My latest request for this vital information produced nothing more than the usual polite promise to "look into the matter." It was quite clear that we were to be as well furnished with essential data we had requested for this next hearing as at Hoffa's first parole hearing in 1969.

In view of this type of cooperation, I took matters into my own hands and contacted the Labor Racketeering Section of the Criminal Division for an up-to-date summary on Hoffa. At the same time, the Organized Crime Section was pointedly queried on Hoffa's connections with the underworld.

As the second parole hearing approached, I became increasingly aware of the strings being pulled to get Hoffa out. Rumor had it that Ed Partin, one of the mobsters who had testified against Hoffa in his jury tampering trial, was being bribed to sign an affidavit that he had lied at that time. The promise of presidential immunity for so doing and of a return to Hoffa's good graces were the tempting rewards.

In contrast to the cover-up at the highest levels of government (including the *Justice* Department), some members of the press were busily investigating Hoffa and courageously publishing the facts as they uncovered them. Knowing the pressures I was facing, Pulitzer-Prize-winning reporter Clark Mollenhoff gave me an autographed copy of *Tentacles of Power*, his brilliant

---

* Sheridan, p. 494.

bestselling expose of Jimmy Hoffa. In the front of the book he wrote the following note:

> To George Reed—
> With the hope that this will be helpful in the Hoffa parole matter. Jimmy Hoffa is the heart of organized crime, and I am sure that the Organized Crime Section at Justice would support that thesis.
> Hoffa will control the Teamsters if you let him out.

The Parole Board hearing opened on March 31 in the full glare of national attention. After facing the eager media (who were barred from the proceedings) and answering their probing questions, I entered the hearing room. It was crowded with authorized participants—immediate family and witnesses and legal counsel. I explained to those present that the Board desired to utilize all available information pertaining to the Hoffa case that would assist it in making a fair and equitable decision. We wished to deal justly not only with the principal in the case but with his family and the Union he represented and the public at large.

I vividly remember how Hoffa's attorney, Rufus King, led off with an impassioned appeal based on Mrs. Hoffa's fragile health. He described her as an "old-fashioned mother-wife type," a "homebody" whose ill health (she was presently hospitalized with a heart condition) was the direct result of her husband's trials and tribulations. King earnestly expressed the opinion that Mrs. Hoffa's only hope for recovery would be if she could be reunited with her husband. Hoffa's speedy release was thus presented as the key to prolonging his wife's life.

As an important part of his plea, King presented a letter

from an executive of the American Trucking Association which attested to Hoffa's "good character and integrity." In courteous but persuasive terms he cited the aggregate 13-year term imposed by Judge Austin in contrast to the five-year term to which his predecessor, Dave Beck, was sentenced, and Beck's parole after serving half his sentence. Again he reiterated Hoffa's need to return to his wife before it was too late.

King took on a tougher tone when he alluded in more detail to Hoffa's "trials and tribulations"—the years of investigations, the indictments, the trials, the newshounds, the press releases, the unremitting fight for his life. Admittedly, Hoffa was as tough as they come. He was a "fighter," fighting for his union and his life, an underdog hero.

At this point Hoffa's attorney strategically changed his tactics. He admitted the "odious" nature of the crime for which his client had been convicted, but hastened to downplay the jury tampering as much less reprehensible when compared with other similar cases. And then there was the matter of Ed Partin and his sworn affidavit: The insinuation was that one man, and a crook at that, had done Hoffa in by his testimony.

Morris Schenker, Hoffa's chief legal counsel, drove that point home with the assertion that the only way the government could have convicted Hoffa was through Partin. Schenker argued that Partin, facing kidnapping, rape, and other charges, simply decided that the government wanted Hoffa more than it wanted him, and that he could buy his own release by testifying against his former boss. It was as simple as that.

With a final expression of confidence in the fairness of the Board, Schenker sat down. The memory of this, one of the most important hearings in my career, remains clear to this day.

James Hoffa, Jr., Jimmy's only son, and a lawyer, next had his say. He dwelt on the hardships of separation for this "very close-knit family," especially as they affected his mother. Her coronary problems, he claimed, were directly related to his father's situation.

James Jr.'s sister referred to her eight-year-old daughter, who had no recollection of her grandfather, and to her mother's seriously ill and sedated condition. She portrayed her parents as a "very devoted couple" who had given their children a perfect example of an ideal marriage. It was a gracious and moving testimony from an obviously devoted daughter. But what did this have to do with justice and the protection of the public? Those important issues had hardly been addressed. And then there was also the matter of union control.

"Attorney King. . . I'd be interested in your addressing a few comments as to Mr. Hoffa's plans for the future— as briefly as you can." I hoped I was being understood. There were vital issues that needed to be faced in this parole hearing.

The response was circuitous and ended ambivalently. He implied that the decision of future leadership was something no one could predict and ought to be left in the hands of the union. He passed this major issue off as though it were unimportant in relation to the more "personal" matters.

"I was just wondering," I pressed, "what his work plans were for the future."

His rambling response was finally focused on what I had expected—and couldn't accept. Hoffa had spent so many years of his life in the labor movement and was so devoted to that cause. Surely there should be some legitimate and appropriate avenues open for him to continue to contribute to the movement.

When the session reconvened that afternoon, I called

upon a top official in the Organized Crime Division to take the stand. What followed was a withering 18-page recital of Jimmy Hoffa's underworld connections compiled from the files of the Organized Crime and Racketeering Section. There was John Diogardi, three times convicted for labor racketeering. There was Joseph Glimco, twice arrested for murder, crony of the Capone gang indicted on shakedown charges among Chicago's merchants and trustee of that city's cabdrivers' Local 77. Hoffa had chosen to ignore an order by court-appointed monitors to suspend his friend Glimco from office and union membership.

There was also Anthony Provenzano, who as International Vice President of the Teamsters was identified by the FBI as having close ties with the Vito Genovese organized crime family. He had been sentenced to seven years on an extortion charge, while his brother, also a union official, had been indicted for counterfeiting. The almost endless litany of crimes committed by union officials and detailed in the McClellan report continued in a monotonous procession. And the damning charges included: "improper operation of welfare funds, extortion, stock fraud, bankruptcy fraud, payoffs, and income tax evasion, association with Chicago mobsters . . . ." Such were the activities of Hoffa's associates and friends.

The Senate report on the McClellan Rackets Committee contained this damning declaration:

> The number of these individuals is such as to rule out the possibility of coincidence or to support Hoffa's claim that he acted only out of motivation to rehabilitate criminals who erred once and then found the path of righteousness . . . .

James R. Hoffa pushed his way into the

presidency of the Teamsters International with
their active support and assistance.

Most germane to the decision that would have to result
from the hearing was the report's conclusion: "The
Committee finds that Hoffa does not now have nor has
he ever had any intention of moving against his racketeer
friends." In all, there had been 203 federal and state
indictments and 127 convictions of Teamster officials and
their associates between January 1961 and May 1965.

In presenting the evidence from the McClellan report,
those representing the Organized Crime Division
explained to the Board that since the Committee's final
report in 1960 to the time of Mr. Hoffa's imprisonment
in 1967, Hoffa had shown no inclination either to rid the
Union of racketeering or to sever his connections with
organized crime. Moreover, in their opinion, not only
had the named racketeers aided in putting Hoffa at the
head of the Teamsters, but these same men had been
rewarded from Teamster pension funds. There was also
indication that Hoffa even now appeared to be in opera-
tional control of the Teamsters while in Lewisburg Federal Prison.

Faced with the evidence, we seven members of the
Parole Board voted unanimously to deny parole to James
Hoffa, an announcement that made headlines throughout
the nation.

One week after the Board's decision, Hoffa walked
unescorted out of Lewisburg Prison and boarded a plane
for San Francisco, where he was being allowed the
unusual privilege of an Easter weekend with his wife, who
was at the University of California Medical Center there.
Hoffa had no sooner arrived at the San Francisco Hilton
than Teamster leaders from all over the country began
converging quietly for what appeared to be a summit

meeting. Though one of the conditions for Hoffa's temporary release had been that he was not to discuss union business while he was out, the identities of the alleged participants were no secret and were meticulously cited by one of the nation's major newspapers. Apparently Jimmy was still his own man and ran his business as he saw fit.

In May, with Hoffa back in prison, I came under intensified pressure. The official high in the Justice Department who had sat next to me on the plane called me into his office on a matter "important to the Attorney General and the White House." He reminded me of our conversation while seated next to each other aboard the Detroit-bound flight in February, when I had shared my personal views regarding the conditions which Hoffa would have to meet before I would consider voting for parole. He reminded me of the large campaign contribution contingent upon getting Hoffa released before the next Teamster convention, scheduled for May 1971. My standard reply to such implications now seemed almost monotonous in its repetitiveness: "I can't permit the Parole Board's decision to be influenced by any political considerations."

Four months after Hoffa's second bid for parole was turned down, his case was again before the Board of Parole. It was there legitimately, thanks to a petition filed by Hoffa's son declaring that his father had notified the International Executive Board of Teamsters that he would not be a candidate for reelection as its President and that he had endorsed a candidate for replacement. In line with Parole Board policies, the petition was found to contain sufficient new evidence to warrant reopening the case and a new hearing. A date was set for August 20.

With the November elections drawing near, the administration's pressure upon me increased. The message couldn't have been plainer, and I got it loudly and clearly from the same official high within the Justice Department: Hoffa's resignation made it imperative that the Board set Jimmy free. When I gave him no grounds for optimism, I was sent to the office of Deputy Attorney General Kleindienst, a colleague for whom I had always entertained the profoundest respect. I reviewed the Hoffa case for him, as requested, and concluded by stating my opinion that the alleged resignation was a farce and that he had no intention of cutting his ties with his mobster friends nor of playing straight with Teamster pension funds.

The response was low-key and friendly but followed the party line: Hoffa's release would not compromise the integrity of the Board and it would be of great help in reelecting President Nixon.

Clearly I was a difficult customer, as I was next shunted upstairs to see Attorney General John Mitchell himself. The message was unequivocal: It was imperative that the Board release Hoffa if Nixon were to be reelected in 1971. The crucial Teamster vote and the equally crucial Teamster money would only be unleashed if Hoffa walked out of Lewisburg: "Your Board will follow your lead, George, if you support his release. They respect your judgment." I could have been flattered by Mitchell's words, but I wasn't. A sickening revulsion for all that this parley stood for swept over me as I heard myself repeat the familiar words about "independent decisions" and "freedom from political pressures." Though I knew it meant my career, there was no question of compromise.

"Mr. Mitchell," I asked, "would you care to see a transcript of the Organized Crimes Section's testimony given at the August hearing?" He demurred, but hastened to remind me of his loyal support for my reappointment as Parole Chairman and his full support for increased budgets and new parole legislation. It was all true, and I appreciated it more than I could express. Until this moment he had kept his promise never to attempt to influence the Parole Board's decision on any case. Now, however, he and Nixon felt I owed them this one favor. It seemed, in his eyes at least, such an incredibly small concession to make in view of the greater good that would ensue for the nation.

It was one of those moments that one would like to walk away from. Perhaps it was true, as Kleindienst had said, that giving in on this one issue wouldn't compromise the integrity of the Board, but I couldn't escape an inner conviction that the facts, not political expediency, must dictate the outcome of the case. Still, I attempted to put the best possible complexion on their maneuvers. I quietly suggested that if John Mitchell, Richard Kleindienst, and Richard Nixon fully reviewed the Hoffa file, they would unanimously vote to deny parole. Mitchell knew it was my final word and brought our meeting to a hasty close. As we took a strained leave of one another, I felt a chill settle over my spirit. I knew that a warm and long-standing relationship had been irretrievably broken.

I returned to my office drained, both physically and emotionally. It was clear that unless we paroled Hoffa at the third hearing on August 20, my standing with the Attorney General and the President would be nonexistent. I also knew I could not act against my convictions. After nearly an hour of self-examination and agonized prayer, a still, small voice spoke the familiar words of comfort to my heart: "Fear God but fear no man." It wasn't, after all, for me to speculate about the outcome, but to abandon myself to God's leading—and His mercy. Warmed in spirit and reassured that God was in control even in this painful crisis, I left my office and drove home.

As the third parole hearing approached, media speculation escalated that *this* time Hoffa—and Nixon—would
have it their way. My response to the ever-pursuing press
hounds was a standard "The decision will be made by
the entire membership of the Parole Board."

Hoffa was represented at his third hearing by his lawyer
son, James Jr. Predictably, he led off with a plea on behalf
of his mother and her need to have her husband at her
side. Having resigned from the leadership of the Teamsters, he would devote himself to her care and recovery
and other personal affairs.

Questioning then focused on pension arrangements
between Hoffa and the Teamsters. Reluctantly, young
Hoffa admitted that his father had already been paid, by
agreement with his Board of Directors, 1.7 million dollars
on this score, although the requested record of negotia-
tions and written agreement pertaining to this sum was
never submitted.

Further questioning disclosed that, as Director of
Membership Drives, Mrs. Hoffa had been paid a yearly
salary of 48,000 dollars for the past 11 years. No duties
were defined. Because of ill health she would, of course,
have been able to fulfill them only in a limited way at
best, and of late not at all. Attorney Hoffa himself had
disclaimed any official relationship with the Teamsters
at the March hearing, even though his law firm received
30,000 dollars per year as a retainer fee and this very day
he stood before us, by his own admission, as that union's
attorney!

Hoffa's future with the Teamsters came under scrutiny.
Just one month before, Hoffa had had bestowed upon him
the title of "President Emeritus of the Teamsters." What
powers, if any, did this new title entail? And what would
prevent Hoffa, once out, from changing his mind and
running for reelection at some time in the future? His

son's disavowals were not reassuring; they ran counter to information we were picking up elsewhere. Neither were his disclaimers as to any knowledge of his father's links with organized crime figures reassuring. They "never discussed" such matters, he insisted.

Cries of "double-cross" met the announcement late that afternoon that Hoffa's third bid for parole had failed. Not only were the Parole Board and more specifically its chairman under fire, but the Hoffa camp cried foul against Mitchell and Nixon for making a "deal" to free Hoffa if he resigned the presidency and then not keeping their end of the bargain. A major newspaper labeled Hoffa a "political prisoner" and called for the formation of a "national committee to free James Riddle Hoffa."

On December 23 President Nixon signed an executive grant of clemency for James Hoffa, commuting his 13-year sentence to 6½ years. All usual procedures which normally take months had been dispensed with. Nixon's signature made Hoffa eligible for immediate release. By the time I heard about it in the office of Norm Carlson, Director of the Bureau of Prisons, Hoffa had already walked out of Lewisburg. I noted that the documents of release, as normally required, did not provide for Parole Board supervision for the remainder of the sentence. Hoffa was a free man as of that day.

In an editorial of December 24, 1971, *The New York Times* commented:

> It would be nice, but naive, to believe that the spirit of Christmas and James R. Hoffa's unblemished record as a prisoner were the only factors that influenced yesterday's decision by President Nixon to let the former leader of the Teamster Union out of jail. However, the

> evidence has been mounting in recent months
> that Hoffa's release has been a pivotal element
> in the strange love affair between the adminis-
> tration and the two-million-member truckers
> union, ousted from the rest of the labor move-
> ment in 1957 for racketeering domination. . . .
> Mr. Nixon's decision to release him—only four
> months after the United States Parole Board had
> refused to let him out, causes one a bit of
> difficulty to avoid the suspicion that the
> imminence of the 1972 elections was a factor
> in Mr. Nixon's decision.

Although I continued to see Attorney General John
Mitchell on a weekly basis at Justice staff meetings, he
never once spoke to me. Each week the price I had
paid to stand by my sincere convictions was brought
home afresh. Ironically, my last public contact with
my former friend and colleague was at the glamorous
farewell dinner held at the Georgetown Club on the
occasion of his resignation as Attorney General in order
to take charge of President Nixon's reelection campaign. It was to be the "last hurrah" for Justice Department heads and their wives before the tragedy
of Watergate would send many of these comrades to
their political deaths and some to prison. Consummate
politician to the end or merely a reluctant adversary—
I couldn't tell which—that evening Mitchell bade me a
cordial farewell.

Ironically, that was not the end. Little did we know
that the final act in our relationship would be played out
as an aftermath to Watergate, when Mitchell himself
would face me as a suppliant in his own parole hearing.

As for Hoffa, the day came when he may have wished

fervently that he had remained in prison. The details of his fate unknown, he vanished in 1975. Who could doubt that his demise was at the hands of his former partners in crime.

16
Hostages to Terrorism

The life of the law has not been logic: it has
been experience.
—Oliver Wendell Holmes, 1881

Declaring that crime has created an unprecedented
"reign of terror" in American cities, Chief Justice Warren
E. Burger, in an address to the American Bar Association
on February 8, 1981, called for a "damage control
program" to deal with what he described as a fight "as
much a part of our national defense as the Pentagon
budget." No matter that an adequate program would be
costly; inaction would be costlier still. Crime, Burger
went on to say, was reducing the United States to the
status of "an impotent society whose capability of maintaining an elementary security on the streets, in schools,
and for the homes of our people is in doubt."

The Chief Justice then turned his attention to the
damning facts. More than one-quarter of all households
in America were being victimized by some kind of criminal activity at least once per year. "Our rate of casual,

day-by-day terrorism in almost any large city exceeds the casualties of all the reported international terrorists in any given year," Burger drove home. Why then, he asked, "do we show such tolerance for the domestic variety? Are we not hostages within the borders of our own selfstyled enlightened, civilized country?"

For most Americans, especially those living in our largest cities, the rising crime rate has become our nation's single most important domestic issue. The FBI statistics are horrendous. New York City, with the same population as all of Sweden, has 20 times as many homicides. Our nation as a whole has 100 times the burglary rate of Japan. Right now 425,000 human beings are under lock and key.

Chilling in its implications is the recent shift in what triggers much of today's crime. Crimes of passion and those motivated by greed are still with us, but there is an escalating new breed of crime—the casual drive-by shootings, the proof-of-manhood killings required of gang initiates, the kill-for-thrills murders that so often drag on as "serial" killings and effectively paralyze the flow of community and city life.

A new threat to the security of families was reported by *The San Diego Union* in its August 15, 1983, edition. "A phenomenon long seen largely in Europe," it reported, "has hit California's affluent Orange County: kidnapping and extortion aimed at wealthy executives. Up to twenty company officers or their families may be held for ransom or hit by extortion each month in the county, which is home to many top executives, security consultants say. Executives . . . fear for their families' safety if they go to the police."

While there is little disagreement on the magnitude of our nation's descent into lawlessness, there is vast disagreement as to where the fault lies and even more as to the solution. Echoing his own Supreme Court opinions, Chief Justice Burger warned before the assembled lawyers of the Bar Association, that the constitutional balance had clearly tipped too far in favor of the criminal defendant and against the victim, and thus society at large.

"A true miscarriage of justice, whether twenty, thirty or forty years old, should always be open to review," Burger stated, "but the judicial progress becomes a mockery of justice if it is forever open to appeals and retrials of error in the arrest, the search, or the trial. Our search for justice must not be twisted into a search for technical errors." He quoted Judge Henry Friendly of the U.S. Court of Appeals as writing that "guilt is not irrelevant" and the late Justice Robert Jackson of the Supreme Court as having reminded us that "the Constitution was not intended to be a suicide pact."

Burger long oposed the so-called "exclusionary rule" and other legal doctrines that prohibit criminal convictions from standing when errors, even technical ones, are committed by police or the courts. For, as he asked the lawyers, "Is a society redeemed if it provides massive safeguards for accused persons, including pre-trial freedom for most crimes, defense lawyers at public expense, trials and appeals, retrials and more appeals almost without end, and yet fails to provide elementary protection for its decent, law-abiding citizens? Trials should be conducted," he declared, "within weeks of arrest" and appeals from conviction "within eight weeks of final judgment."

Although the man on the street (or, more accurately barricaded behind locked doors) would have applauded, the reaction of the American Civil Liberties Union was as expected. Barely an hour after the Chief Justice finished his speech, a representative of this overseer of the nation's liberties appeared in the convention press room with a strongly worded critique of Burger's "simplistic" proposals.

My experience in administering the federal parole system for almost a quarter of a century brings me into close alignment with Chief Justice Burger's opinion that a "war on crime" in this country is long overdue. The courts have failed miserably to protect society by failing to provide the greatest deterrents to crime: a speedy trial (as the Constitution guarantees), the certainty of penalty, and the finality of judgment. The judicial process mocks justice if any of the three are lacking. That all three are all too often missing is in itself a travesty of justice.

The willful failure of courts to protect society from its criminal elements has created a crisis of confidence in our nation's judicial system. For this the Supreme Court's liberal majority during Chief Justice Earl Warren's tenure (along with the state courts which have extended its decisions) must accept the blame. The maze of constantly shifting procedural rules which that court spewed forth for the better part of 25 years was responsible for keeping on or returning to the streets a host of criminals without adequate regard for their guilt or the security and safety of law-abiding citizens.

In addition to the problems raised by Chief Justice Burger in the administration of the criminal justice system, society also suffers because of the widespread policy of plea bargaining. When a prosecutor has weak evidence in a case, overworked staff, or political ambitions, he often strikes a deal with the accused to either lessen the severity of the charges or drop some of the counts entirely in exchange for his willing cooperation on the witness stand and his agreement to plead guilty to a lesser charge.

Another of the many factors crippling the criminal justice system is the enormous disparity in sentencing practices throughout the nation. In multiple-judge federal courts, the length of the sentence handed down often depends upon the courtroom to which the defendant is assigned. With a total lack of any guidelines for sentencing in either federal, state, or local courts, one must conclude that neither the cause of justice relative to the felon nor the cause of protection for our citizens is being served.

Capital punishment, society's ultimate weapon in punishing the capital offender, remains a hotly contested issue. It is hardly a creation of modern society. Capital punishment was an accepted form of punishment under early English law, and the framers of our own Bill of Rights expressly recognized its use in the Fifth Amendment. While capital punishment had its opponents, its legitimacy has never until recent times been seriously questioned by the U.S. Supreme Court.

The decade of the sixties, however, changed all that. As debate among lawmakers and the public escalated, the number of executions decreased dramatically. Between 1950 and 1959, 708 persons were executed nationwide. That number dropped to 188 between 1960 and 1965. Then there was a virtual moratorium: Between 1965 and 1972 there were only three executions in the entire nation. Clearly the courts reflected the nation's mounting attention to civil rights issues and vastly expanding rights for defendants and convicted felons, and simply stopped carrying out death sentences.

It was in this climate of increased leniency toward the criminal that, in 1972, the nation's highest court declared capital punishment unconstitutional. The Furman decision was close and was lacking in harmony, with only five of the nine justices voting to strike down the supreme penalty. Two of the five declared that capital punishment was not and never could be constitutional. The other three declined to go so far, expressing instead the view that only existing practices were unconstitutional. The justices complained that the application of the penalty had too often been "arbitrary," "capricious," and "freakish" because there were insufficient guidelines to help judges and juries make life-versus-death decisions. Virtually the only point of agreement among the five was that the death penalty had fallen with undue severity on minorities and the poor.

A bare four years later, on July 2, 1976, the U.S. Supreme Court again ruled on the constitutionality of the death penalty, this time declaring that execution is not "cruel and unusual punishment" (which is of course forbidden by the Constitution). The opinion of the court was expressed as follows:

> We hold that the death penalty is not a form of punishment that may never be imposed, regardless of the circumstances of the offense, regardless of the character of the offender, and regardless of the procedure followed in reaching the decision.

States were now expected to write into their death penalty statutes specific standards which would eliminate the "arbitrariness and caprice" of the laws which the high court had struck down in 1972. It had never intended to impose a ban on all executions per se, it implied, but wished to make sure that states would clarify, by law, the kinds of aggravating or mitigating circumstances that would make sentencing a more evenhanded instrument of justice.

Thirty-five states responded promptly by writing new death-penalty statutes. No doubt a major motivation was the hope that speedy reinstatement of the supreme penalty would help to quell a crime wave gone out of control. FBI statistics showed that there had been a consistent increase after 1965 of violent and assaultive crimes being perpetrated upon all segments of society. The only question remaining was whether these new statutes would meet the Supreme Court standards.

The states' haste to comply with the Supreme Court's new fiat also seemed to reflect a strong backlash of public opinion in favor of the extreme penalty. A sense of moral outrage in the face of particularly heinous and reprehensible crimes seemed now the "righteous" social response.

The 1976 Supreme Court decision did not immediately put all 588 men and women on death row in jeopardy of their lives. On the contrary, the Court tried five cases simultaneously in five states in order to test the constitutionality of state laws and thus set minimum procedural standards for death penalty states. As a result, a number of the new state statutes were voided. Significantly, North Carolina was one of the states whose laws were considered too stringent in making death mandatory for certain crimes; that state accounted for 109 of the 588 men on death row. The high court made clear its intention that capital punishment must be limited to only the most serious offenses and that it must be applied by what the court termed a process of "guided discretion." In plain language, the court or jury must focus on the facts of the offense and the defendant's criminal and social history.

After a decade of turmoil, capital punishment was again legal. By the end of 1978, 34 states and the federal government had new or revised capital-punishment laws. According to government surveys, the vast majority of these laws complied with all prescribed constitutional standards. As a result, in California alone the number of death-status inmates jumped from nine at the end of 1978 to 25 by the end of the following year.

What the future holds in practical results, however, is difficult to assess, for, as was true in 1972, the death row population has increased, but executions have remained a rarity. If the chief lawmakers are unwilling to enforce the death penalty (as much of the public perceives to be the case in California's high court), they may find themselves in direct political conflict with an aroused and angry public that will spare no energy to make the courts more responsive to public opinion and public safety.

Ideally, only such considerations as a just sentencing for the offender, effective rehabilitation, and the protection of society at large should influence the administration of the justice system. That this is not so is hardly a secret. Two factors that have exerted great pressure for the acquittal or early release of dangerous men and women have been our outdated prison system and our overcrowded facilities. With our prison population expanding 15 times as fast as the national population, the overwhelming question is no longer how to effectively lodge them but simply *where*. So grave has the situation become that in 1976 U.S. Judge Frank Johnson ruled that conditions in the Alabama State prisons were so inhumane that they violated the Eighth Amendment prohibiting cruel and unusual punishment. A convicted felon in that state's facilities could expect nothing better than a six-man, bedless, lightless, waterless cell with a hole in the floor.

The reason for such subhuman conditions can be found partly in our escalating crime rate. From 1968 to 1978 the prison population in the United States jumped by almost two-thirds, to more than 300,000. In California, our most populous state, more than 90,000 persons per year are arrested in connection with about 200,000 crimes. It would be impossible to convict even a significant fraction of these people because, with facilities for only about 30,000 prisoners, there would simply be no place to put them. Building more facilities, the obvious answer, becomes prohibitive, with present prison construction costs now exceeding 100,000 dollars per bed. At this price, the housing for only a small facility holding 1000 inmates would mean a cost to the taxpayers of 100 million dollars! The ongoing per-annum cost of housing, care, and supervision for one prison inmate is twice that of keeping a student at Harvard! The State of California presently spends more than three *billion* dollars annually to administer its criminal justice system. Would its citizens be willing to spend more—much more—to do the job right? Would they be willing to commit their pocketbooks to the task, even though there are a multitude of worthy programs competing for a place in federal and state budgets, each seemingly more urgent than the last?

Criminals who live as public enemies usually begin prison life with a deep resentment against "society" for putting them there, and are in turn quickly embittered by real or imaginary deficiencies in prison facilities. Sometimes that resentment explodes in violence and destruction, as it did at the New Mexico State Penitentiary near Santa Fe early in February 1980. At its dedication in 1954, the prison had been lauded as one of the most advanced correctional institutions in the world.

Administrative turnover (five wardens in five years) and overcrowding nullified all the plans and projections that looked so good on paper. At the time of the uprising, described by *Newsweek* as "one of the most brutal prison riots in U.S. history," 1136 prisoners were jammed into space designed for 800. Besides the overcrowding, inmates had often registered complaints about rats in their cells, roaches in their food, and rough treatment by guards, who apparently were underpaid, poorly trained, and too few in number.

Strangely enough, when the seething rage at last exploded, no guards were killed, though many were taken hostage. Instead, the prisoners went on a 36-hour rampage of sadistic violence against each other that included beheading, hanging, torching, and rape. When the carnage was over, 33 inmates had died. It was a frightening display of uncontrolled fury that "turned everybody into animals," according to one 21-year-old inmate who was locked naked in a room, tied, gagged, hooded and raped at least ten times. The terror was so pervasive that prisoners fought to give themselves up to the police. Eventually 700 succeeded in doing so.

Some nine years earlier, on September 9, 1971, one of the bloodiest prison riots in the history of American penology broke loose at the Attica Maximum Security State Prison in New York State. Governor Rockefeller had gone to great effort to hire Russell Oswald, my longtime friend (who was trained in the very permissive Wisconsin correctional program) to serve as the Commissioner of New York State's vast penal system. Commissioner Oswald, when he tried to "open up" an old-line prison system, found out that once the Pandora's box of "prisoners' rights" is opened just a little, there is no stopping the flood tide of demands. Bargaining sessions were held over a period of several days to try to negotiate terms with the self-proclaimed "political prisoners." When all efforts failed, the power of the New York State National Guard, the State Police, and the prison guards crushed the riot, but not without tragic loss of life.

It is a fact upon which both liberals and conservatives agree that our courts and our prison system have failed to do the job of rehabilitation that not too long ago was the great hope of the progressive criminologist. No longer are even liberals so ready to view man as essentially rational, responsible, and altruistic in nature. Neither do they all buy the idea that society has imposed a gridlock of behaviors which in effect "causes" crime and must therefore be "treated" and "cured" like any communicable disease.

Opinions are polarized. Some criminologists declare that the search for the causes of crime is futile and that agents of the state should revert to the age-old practice of merely locking up offenders and imposing equal sentences for equal crimes. Some argue, on the other hand, that all punitive measures should be abandoned and all energies and funds diverted to a study of the causes of crime. Neither the courts nor society at large seem ready to put either extreme to the acid test, and in the meantime crime has escalated to the degree that our citizens live in terror in their own homes, while abroad our credibility as a democratic institution is at risk among the world community of nations.

My own views parallel closely the recent recommendations of the Federal Task Force on Violent Crime. This blue-ribbon panel obviously had the protection of the citizenry in mind when they proposed these measures, among others:

1. Permit judges to deny bail to persons rated as a danger to the community.
2. Allow verdicts of "guilty but mentally ill," thus blocking release of many serious offenders.
3. Make illegally seized evidence admissible in trials if police thought they were complying with the law.
4. Bar lawsuits challenging convictions unless filed

within three years.

5. Impose a mandatory minimum prison sentence for gun use in committing a crime.

6. Step up drug enforcement, using diplomatic pressure on drug-exporting nations and assigning military units to help fight drug smuggling.

7. Prosecute major youth gangs in Federal Court on the grounds that they constitute a form of organized crime.

8. Improve and strengthen the "organized crime" section of the criminal division to fight organized crime in America.

Though supportive of stringent measures such as the foregoing, I also believe that we dare not abandon—indeed, must intensify—our creative efforts in the field of penology. To do that effectively, however, would require 1) a major commitment of resources for the task, 2) adequate staffing to produce presentencing reports that would provide critical insights, 3) diagnostic clinics capable of undertaking a 90-day assessment period for all prisoners, 4) classification committees to place the inmate in the proper training and treatment programs, and 5) legislation of modified-indeterminate-sentence structures providing tough minimum sentences and long maximum sentences for all aggressive and assaultive offenses.

The U.S. Board of Parole's five-year research project, "Improved Parole Decision-Making," laid out the salient factors that could help predict an inmate's success or failure on parole. By proper initial classification we were able to successfully separate the criminal types. Those who were classified as confirmed sociopaths could be placed in maximum security prisons for long periods of incarceration, primarily for the protection of society.

Others, who were able to profit from intense counseling and vocational training, could be given the opportunity of becoming productive members of society while under close parole supervision in the community. Those who had committed nonviolent or situational offenses and had little or no prior criminal record could be placed in small, minimum security, retraining facilities prior to being placed under parole supervision. First-time offenders for whom clinical or academic retraining were not deemed necessary could be placed in forestry camps or similar constructive-labor-type environments designed to rebuild both people and natural resources. A final category involved a community service project in which the inmate could make financial restitution to his victim as well as perform a useful service to his fellow citizens.

Whatever else the criminal justice system does or does not do, I believe that the identification and segregation of dangerous and aggressive prisoners in long-term, maximum security, Alcatraz-type prisons is imperative to the survival of our American society. Felons who have been given every opportunity to rehabilitate themselves in less stringent confinement, but have failed to do so, should be isolated from society until they have completed their maximum terms of imprisonment. A proper and courageous use of the authority delegated by God to governments as His intended instruments of righteousness will again permit our citizens to live in their cities and communities as they were meant to live—without fear.

17
Land of the Free

If my people, which are called by my name,
shall humble themselves, and pray, and seek my
face, and turn from their wicked ways, then
will I hear from heaven, and will forgive their
sin, and will heal their land.

Our nation was born in peril. George Washington,
upon taking command of the new and struggling Colonial
Army on June 15, 1776, was well aware of that fact when
he prayed:

Almighty God: We make our earnest prayer
that Thou wilt incline the hearts of the citizens
to cultivate a spirit of subordination and obedience to government and entertain a brotherly
affection and love for one another and for their
fellow citizens of the United States at large.
And finally that Thou wilt most graciously
be pleased to dispose us all to do justice, to love

mercy, and to demean ourselves with that charity, humility, and pacific temper of mind which were characteristic of the divine Author of our blessed religion, and without a humble imitation of whose example in these things we can never hope to be a happy nation.

Grant our supplication, we beseech thee, through Jesus Christ our Lord. Amen.

On July 4, 1976, 200 years to the day since our Founding Fathers had signed the Declaration of Independence, I was highly honored to address as part of the nation's bicentennial commemoration the Williamsburg, Virginia, Church of the Nazarene at its morning worship service. My subject was "Faith of our Fathers."

As I prepared my address, I was very much aware that my beloved country was again in grave peril. The location of the church where I would be speaking, so very near the Bruton Parish Church where our Founding Fathers had often met to pray for divine leadership during the trying days leading to the break with England and the Revolutionary War, heightened that awareness. The occasion of our nation's 200-year birthday and all the patriotic fervor and retrospection it generated in American hearts and minds helped intensify my feelings as well.

My opening remarks on that memorable Sunday reminded my audience that 3½ centuries before, a small band of 102 Pilgrims had set sail in the *Mayflower* to seek in the New World a place where they could worship God according to the dictates of their own consciences.

A few years before their historic landing on these shores, three small ships with 144 persons aboard had sailed down the Thames and out to the open sea to establish, after a five-month voyage, a small colony at Jamestown, Virginia, just nine miles from where my

252 / Fear No Man

listeners were then seated. In 1699 that small settlement became the capital of the Virginia colony and the future gathering place of the dedicated and freedom-loving champions of an embryo nation.

I referred to the Declaration of Independence and its glorious concluding paragraph. The words so nobly conceived could not fail to move the heart of every American citizen:

> We hold these truths to be self-evident: that all men are created equal, that they are endowed by their Creator with certain unalienable rights: that among these are life, liberty, and the pursuit of happiness; that to secure these rights, governments are instituted among men, deriving their just powers from the consent of the governed; that whenever any form of government becomes destructive of their ends, it is the right of the people to alter or abolish it and to institute a new government, laying its foundation on such principles and organizing its powers in such form as to them seem likely to effect their safety and happiness. . . .
>
> We, therefore, the Representatives of the United States of America, in General Congress assembled, appealing to the Supreme Judge of the world for the rectitude of our intentions, do, in the name and by authority of the good people of these colonies, solemnly publish and declare: that these United Colonies are, and of right ought to be, free and independent States. . . .
>
> And for the support of this Declaration, with a firm reliance on the protection of Divine

Providence, we mutually pledge to each other
our lives, our fortunes, and our sacred honor.

"What a heritage! What a commitment!" I concluded.
Our declaration was indeed a grandly conceived proclamation against the King of England and all would-be
tyrants. Many of the brave men who signed this historic
document would in fact pay dearly in life and property
for their courageous act. Of the 56 signers of the Declaration of Independence, nine died during the course of
the war, five were captured by the British and died a cruel
death under torture, and 12 returned from the war to
the torched ruins of their homes. We had been willing
to pay the price then. Life itself had not been too great
a cost to secure for our children the political and religious freedoms we claimed to espouse.

In spite of our nation's uncertain and tenuous beginning, God had honored the zeal and fortitude and
prayerful vision of its founders. The infant nation
prospered and quickly established itself as a bastion of
freedom and opportunity.

Having defended our shores, however, against those
who would impose their wills upon these United States,
we have not defended our individual rights against those
within our society who would rob us of our lives, our
property, and our rightful and reasonable pursuit of
happiness. "Righteousness exalteth a nation," declared
the wise son of David, "but sin is a reproach to any
people." We dare not risk our very survival, as Rome did,
by submitting to a long, agonizing slide into moral and
civil chaos.

As we look for solutions, we must look to the moral
changes needed for real peace to reign in our cities and
countryside—changes that no amount of money can buy.
The dilemma we face in the area of crime control is of

devastating proportions and seemingly beyond the competence of human ingenuity to solve.

God Himself has named the fatal flaw at the root of man's problem as *sin*. He has also named its cure as Jesus Christ and His life-changing power. Yet mankind seems as little inclined today as throughout the long, agonized drama of human history to avail itself of divine help.

But what of America, the land so fortuitously founded and so signally blessed? What hope do we have of seeing a moral renaissance emerge from the present debacle? General Douglas MacArthur left us a solemn reminder when he stated: "History fails to record a single precedent in which nations subject to moral decay have not passed into political and economic decline. There has been either a spiritual awakening to overcome the moral lapse or a progressive deterioration leading to ultimate national disaster."

Do we see signs of such a spiritual awakening? As in most cases when we are confronted with questions of this nature, the ledger contains entries on both sides. Our history itself pleads the cause of our continuity as a Christian nation. Our Founding Fathers' unabashed declarations of dependence upon God are still a treasured part of our heritage, and one which our people are not ready to relinquish. Neither appeals to the "separation of church and state" doctrine nor ridicule enabled Madalyn Murray O'Hair to arouse public support for her campaign to strike the words "In God we trust" from our coins.

To *trust* God has far deeper implications than the mere presence of such words upon our coinage. The need of the hour, if disaster is to be averted, is for that trust to be exercised in all its intended meanings, and not just as a euphemism to cover the expectation that God will bless this nation's plans, whatever they may be. There is a price to be paid for divine blessing, and that price is always *obedience to divine law*. Otherwise the "trust" in God that we proclaim can only mean a sure expectation of the judgment He has declared against all unrighteousness. The Christian heritage that we acclaim is a fragile treasure that must not be allowed to languish in our nation's history books, but must be sincerely nurtured in this age.

Considerable optimism has been generated lately in the Christian community by the more activist political role being taken by Christians. A 1980 nationwide Gallup Poll reported one in three adults claiming to be born again. A California poll the same year reported one in four of that state's citizens as having had a turning-point experience of committing their lives to Christ. Individuals are seeking public office in order to speak out on moral issues, and coalitions are forming to work for pro-God, pro-life, pro-family policies in government so that, according to *The Conservative Digest,* "clear-cut moral choices can be offered to the voters for the first time in decades." Opinion is being polarized and dialogue becoming heated, but the issues at least are being confronted and Americans are better able to make choices based upon clearly defined alternatives.

Another hopeful sign is the newly emerging view of the criminal mind, one which holds the criminal responsible for his behavior. Too long our prison psychologists have parroted the Freudian concept of delinquent behavior, which he termed "compulsive" and "irresistible" because it derived from a set of primitive and antisocial instincts. Had Freud used the more accurate and more easily understood term which Christian evangelicals use for transgressions of God's laws, Freud would have spared Western man much needless "analysis" and have arrived much more quickly at the cure.

Today we have some courageous criminologists who

are daring to suggest that even the most economically, socially, and emotionally deprived human beings make conscious, rational choices between good and evil behavior. Their voices echo biblical precedent. Israel was exhorted by God through His prophets to *turn* from her evil ways. In an earlier day Moses had warned the multitude at the giving of the Covenant: "I call heaven and earth to record this day against you, that I have set before you life and death, blessing and cursing: therefore choose life. . . ." The choice was not beyond the ability of these men and women to make, for Moses had prefaced the warning with these words: "For this commandment which I command thee this day, it is not hidden from thee, neither is it far off. . . . But the word is very nigh unto thee, in thy mouth, and in thy heart, that thou mayest do it." Joshua, too, on the threshold of the Promised Land, voiced the same challenge to the same people when he cried, "Choose you this day whom ye will serve!"

For twentieth-century man as well, salvation requires a conscious act of turning from the old life and turning to Christ. God does not "accept" our past, commiserate with its shortcomings, or seek to explain the present by the deficiences of childhood. No, He denounces our past, and we must renounce and turn from it too. With that therapeutic and cleansing exercise out of the way, we can proceed to get on with our new lives. How easy prison rehabilitation would be if such an honest acknowledgment of guilt and such a healthy repentance prevailed! We can be encouraged that at least some of today's penologists are taking a second look at the concept of personal responsibility when assessing the criminal mind. Though not accepted for the right reason—that it is biblically sound—it may be the philosophy of the future because it makes sense.

Over the years I have been privileged to observe occasional instances of the only real and lasting rehabilitation known in the prison system—or anywhere, for that matter. It is the kind of rehabilitation that can take a man of raw and self-serving political ambition like Chuck Colson through the crucible of trial, conviction, and prison cell and bring him out on the other side a regenerate, humble servant of Christ and of his fellowman. The Watergate scandal, which brought down a United States President and 25 of my federal colleagues, did incalculable damage to my fellow citizens' trust of all public officials. Colson, through his postprison ministry, has done as much as one man might be expected to do in order to demonstrate the life-changing reality of a jailhouse conversion—and thus to redeem that trust.

God's way, the way that miraculously exchanges the criminal mind and all its destructive impulses for the mind of Christ, is undeniably the best way. That narrow way requires a choice, however, and until men and women are willing to make that deliberate choice of life, they will have to face the same alternative as the throngs who heard its solemn pronouncement from Moses' lips at the giving of the Law. That alternative was *death*—spiritual and ultimately physical.

In the meantime, God's second best must be in force. In the absence of a willing obedience to the laws which under God operate for human benefit, we must revive (or impose under duress) those same God-breathed principles of social order which alone will allow our people to pursue their lives in peace with themselves and with their fellowman.

APPENDIX

BURT LANCASTER

April 6, 1962

Mr. George J. Reed
Board of Parole
101 Indiana Avenue, N. W.
Washington, D. C.

Dear Mr. Reed:

It is my great pleasure to invite you and your guest to join me at a special screening of BIRDMAN OF ALCATRAZ on Wednesday, April 25, at 8:00 p.m. at the Georgetown Theatre, 1351 Wisconsin Avenue, N. W.

A private supper party following the screening, across the street in the Rayburn Room of Billy Martin's Carriage House, 1238 Wisconsin Avenue, N. W., will give us the opportunity to meet once again.

The film, based on the life of one Robert Stroud, is the shocking story of the most defiant man I have ever read or heard about. Your understanding will begin when you read the enclosed material on Stroud, the killer, convict, scholar, scientist. I am convinced that only by showing you the film personally and talking with you could you comprehend my deep involvement, emotionally and intellectually, with this man and his life.

Moreover, you will have the opportunity to meet the two men who have done so much to bring the case of Robert Stroud into world focus, and who are exerting every effort today to free him—Tom Gaddis, a former probation officer whose book, *Birdman of Alcatraz*, first revealed the startling story, and Stanley Furman, who has led in vain the legal battle to make Stroud a free man.

Please reply to Miss Whiston, District 7-0728.

I am looking forward to seeing you very soon.

Sincerely yours,

Burt Lancaster

Parole Better Protects Society

In this day when the total resources of the Western world have been committed to the defense of freedom itself, it is well for us in America not only to take stock of our military strength but to reevaluate our total resources. This includes a new look not only at our supply of steel, oil, wheat, or atomic bombs but a look at our human resources as well. If we are to emerge final victors over the power of the Kremlin, it will require that we make full use of our "front-line fighting men" and that we also make every effort to salvage some of the less capable and less desirable raw material.

Business and industrial leaders have traditionally attempted to make the optimum use of our best minds to improve our products and standard of living. We have planned complex personnel systems in order to get the most good out of the most people. Over the past twenty years in my career as a Federal and State official in the field of corrections, I have seen a parade of persons whom many look upon as the waste product of our society. We in the field of corrections take a different approach, however, to those men and women who have run afoul of our laws. We feel that they are not always waste material, but that these people represent a vast pool of untapped energy.

Throughout the centuries man has attempted to find a means of controlling the law-violator. He has done this through exile and ostracism; he has done this by cutting off the offending member of the criminal body (the tongue of a traitor, the hand of a thief, and the eyes of a Peeping Tom); and he has done this by executioner's block or firing squad. Despite these measures, however, none of these methods used throughout our history has resulted in any substantial decrease in crime. Indeed, national statistics reveal that crime is an ever-increasing phenomenon of our present-day world.

Until the last century mankind has done precious little to control the behavior of the law-violator after he has been incarcerated. We have experimented with behavior control and rehabilitation behind bars in a rigidly controlled situation. Now at last we are actually doing something about control and rehabilitation after a law-violator is declared safe enough to return to society. We no longer need merely to hope that he has "learned his lesson." Now we supervise him and observe him while he is in prison to see whether he is heading toward respectable citizenship and whether he is acquiring an attitude of self-respect and the feeling that law violation is beneath his dignity. Through this observation there is possibly a selection of certain persons suitable for release under conditions prior to the time that sentence would normally expire.

We must realize that although we sometimes become absorbed in TV and movie shows in which the criminal is relentlessly tracked down by police and the judge's gavel strikes as he pronounces sentence during the closing seconds of the episode, in actual life this is not the end of the story. The real story of the criminal is only beginning at this stage. Ninety-seven percent of all committed prisoners return to the community—most of them within a relatively short time. In the Federal system the average prisoner's release occurs, except for capital offenses, after a little more than three years of imprisonment. These persons return with either an institutional experience to guide their behavior or with added controls provided by a field officer and the officials of a parole system. It goes without saying, except in those instances where a prisoner would chafe and be made unduly rebellious, that the added controls of parole increase his chances for successful living.

A parolee agrees, as a condition of his release, to abide by a set of established rules of conduct. One of these is that he will commit no further crimes. Several other conditions control his movement, require him to remain steadily employed, if possible, and make imperative regular personal reporting to his supervisor, who guides and sometimes prods him into socially acceptable deportment. Thus the long step from prison living to being an accepted member of his community is aided through the parole system.

I further contend that it is downright cruel to turn a man out through the iron gate without someone to whom he can turn for help and guidance. Release from prison is a psychological shock. We must provide something to ease that shock, or else the consequences might be disastrous not only to the man himself but to other members of society as well.

In addition to the types of controls mentioned earlier, parole provides retraining. The return to crime is usually greatest during the first few months following release. It is during this period that the individual who has been locked away from normal community life is less capable of adjusting to the demands of society. It is then that he must undergo a severe and rapid reappraisal of his own thinking as he encounters pressures from the outside. The assistance offered by professional parole workers during this crucial time often spells the difference between the return to a criminal life or to respectable citizenship.

Rehabilitation definitely is taking place in prisons where diagnosis and treatment regimens are well staffed and programmed, but this is necessarily limited to the controlled environment, with only limited free choice permitted. The acid test comes after release. During the parole period the rehabilitation and retraining is accomplished in the actual setting in which the individual's life will be lived. Parole, therefore, is a serving of part of the sentence in the community and is an integral part of the correctional process—all of which is geared to the rehabilitation of the individual.

Parole is a selective process designed to make available technical supervision to those persons who will profit from it. There are those who suggest that every prisoner who is not a threat to society should be released under parole. I must say, however, that until sufficient numbers of trained field personnel and the funds to attract and retain that personnel are available—and further, that until the majority of the general public wholeheartedly accepts the philosophy of parole—the Board of Parole must select those prisoners who can best use the available resources. For these reasons the United States Board of Parole has over the past few years granted parole to approximately one-third of those prisoners who make application.

The measure and quality of the selective process may be better evaluated in the number of paroled prisoners who complete their parole period without incident. I am happy to report that for the past several years, 80 percent of the Federal prisoners who were released on parole successfully completed their supervision periods. What is more, of the remaining 20 percent who were returned as a result of violations, 5 percent were returned not because of further law violations but because of so-called "administrative violations" of the conditions imposed by the Board. This latter group of violators was returned as a preventive measure, and if the parole process had not been functioning, that 5 percent might later have committed further acts of crime. Here again, parole serves in a very real manner as a protection to society.

It concerns me at times to see parole being confused with other forms of release. Newsmen as well as the public generally tend to confuse the terms in use by correctional officials. Much of this is our own fault, and we hasten to clear up this confusion as rapidly as possible. You may or may not know that even in the absence of parole, most prisoners are released under conditions prior to expiration of sentence. These releases are the result of "good time" earned by good behavior in the institution. This form of release has nothing to do with parole, and prisoners so released are a type of prisoner apart from parolees. Parolees are selected by a board. The others are released according to statutory provisions, which often include a schedule for good-time credits. Those releases are mandatory by law. In the Federal system we now call such persons "mandatory releasees" as opposed to parolees. There is still a third class of prisoner, who is released neither by mandatory release nor by parole but is let out upon expiration of sentence without any conditions or supervision of any kind.

An instance of this confusion in newspapers and magazines was recently brought to my attention when a colleague of mine pointed out a portion of the August, 1958, issue of a leading detective magazine. This article stated that when a certain resident of the Los Angeles area was serving time in a Federal prison that—and I quote—"all Mickey had to do was behave himself and wait for his parole. It came finally on September 5, 1955." I strongly protest this statement, and for the record I state that Mickey Cohen was not granted parole. The United States Board of Parole heard his case upon his application and denied his plea in 1953. He was actually released on mandatory release, as required by statute, more than two years later. This is the type of reporting that retards the true and full understanding of parole as a means of control and retraining for those individuals who can profit from the services available.

Members of the press and representatives of mass news media usually make a very real effort to be accurate in reporting facts. They, as well as movie and TV writers and producers, can perform a great community service by educating the public to a better understanding of the value and nature of parole. I know that our own semantics have at times been misleading, but at the present time we have a fairly uniform terminology. Parole officials will always be happy to check out an ex-prisoner's actual status before providing undeserved ammunition to those critics who would revert to the old practice of "lock 'em up and when they're sorry turn 'em loose."

Yes, parole better protects society and is an enlightened method for releasing, under supervision, prisoners from a correctional institution. However, when a prisoner who has made excellent progress during his incarceration faces the problems of his job, hostile neighbors, and the inquiring eyes of his own family, the pressure is sometimes too great, and he may return to a life of crime. We therefore need to better educate our community and industrial leaders, personnel directors, and social agencies to solicit their assistance in helping cushion this traumatic experience for the newly released prisoner.

Some three years ago the National Exchange Club launched an imaginative and challenging program to assist youths committed under the Federal Youth Corrections Act. This project, known as the National Exchange Club Sponsorship Program, was set up to get Exchangites all over the country to help secure jobs and homes or just act as "big brother" to youths released on parole. This program was launched under the very able leadership of my good friend, past National President Harold Mott, and has had the constant support of his successors as well as our National Secretary, Mr. Herold Harter. The present Chairman of the Youth Correction Division of the United States Board of Parole, Mr. Louis J. Grout, fully concurs with me that this program is a very important service to our youthful offenders, and I know that our Board will continue to give full support to this most worthwhile activity.

The project has had some growing pains and has developed some problems in getting organized. Many Exchange Clubs have gone to a great deal of trouble to set up administrators and have not yet håd any youths referred to them for assistance. It will take a period of time for our local United States Probation and Parole Officers as well as institutional personnel to become familiar with the program. But already many reports have come to our attention in which Exchangites have been of great help to our parolees in making a satisfactory adjustment in the home community. Other clubs have called in the local Federal and State correctional personnel to explain their programs, thus making a real contribution to this problem of educating the local community to a better understanding of what they can do to improve correctional programs.

For the past twenty years I have been privileged to see many advances in the field of corrections, and I am proud to have been a small part of this program. But I am convinced that professionals working alone can never successfully meet the ever-increasing tide of crime in our nation today. We must find ways of better interpreting our objectives, our programs, and our problems to the public generally if we are to have their badly needed support and assistance in meeting a very real threat to an orderly society.

---

* Speech given before the National Exchange Club Convention in Los Angeles, California. Published in *Vital Speeches of the Day; United States Congressional Record*, Washington, D. C. and *The National Exchange Club Magazine, The Exchangite.*